EVIL, SUFFERING AND RELIGION

Issues in Religious Studies

GENERAL EDITORS

Professor Peter Baelz and Jean Holm

Further titles in this series

EVIL,
SUFFERING AND RELIGION

Brian Hebblethwaite

SHELDON PRESS
LONDON

First published in Great Britain in 1976 by
Sheldon Press, Marylebone Road, London NW1 4DU

Printed in Great Britain by
Northumberland Press Limited, Gateshead

ISBN 0 85969 097 0

CONTENTS

BRIAN HEBBLETHWAITE was born in Bristol in 1939 and took degrees in Classics and Philosophy and Theology from Oxford and Cambridge. He was ordained and served his curacy in a Lancashire cotton town. He returned to Cambridge as Chaplain of Queens' College and is now Fellow and Dean of Chapel there. He has been an Assistant Lecturer in Divinity in the University of Cambridge since 1973.

Issues in Religious Studies

GENERAL PREFACE TO THE SERIES

This series of books offers an introduction to some of the central issues involved in religious studies. It aims to be as dispassionate as possible, assuming a serious interest on the part of the reader but neither previous study in the area nor commitment to any religious position. It seeks to combine a basic rigour of thought with a concreteness of approach.

The purpose of each book is to indicate the nature of the issue, the questions raised by it, and the main directions in which thinkers have looked for answers to such questions. It should thus provide a firm foundation on which further study can be built.

The series was designed in the first place to meet the needs of students embarking on courses in religious studies in colleges of education and universities, and of senior pupils following the revised 'A' level syllabuses. However, the books are not in any narrow sense 'text books', and it is hoped that they will be of value to anyone approaching a study of these issues for the first time.

PETER BAELZ AND JEAN HOLM

PREFACE

The problem of evil is one of the main stumbling-blocks to a religious view of the world. In this book I survey the different ways in which the religions of the world have attempted to cope with the problem, both practically and theoretically. At the same time, I try not only to describe but to discuss their different approaches, pointing out their scope, and examining their rationality. In carrying out this double task, I aim to show the fruitfulness for Religious Studies of a combination of the two disciplines known as the Comparative Study of Religions and the Philosophy of Religion. The largeness of the topic and the brevity of the treatment inevitably involve some oversimplification, but I hope that this book will serve as an introduction to more thorough study of the nature and resources of religion over against the world's evil.

I am grateful to the editors of this series and to my colleague Dr J. J. Lipner for their very helpful comments on the first draft of this book.

1

THE BUDDHA AND THE KARAMAZOVS

THE BUDDHA

The story is told of the Buddha that, as the prince Siddhartha Gautama, he was kept by his father the King in the upper rooms of the palace, so that he should never see anything that could upset him. There he was entertained by music and dancing and the sweet delights of women's company. But the women told him of the pleasant groves in the countryside near the city, and Gautama determined to go outside the palace to see them for himself. The King allowed such excursions, giving orders, however, that all those with any kind of affliction should be kept away from the prince's route. Notwithstanding these instructions, Gautama met on his excursions first an old man, then a man with a diseased body, and thirdly a corpse. Thus the prince became acquainted with the facts of senility, disease and death, and was awakened to the impermanence of everything in this world. He was filled with dismay and anxiety; he became disillusioned with the pleasures of the senses, and resolved to abandon them. He left the palace and, overcome with grief for the suffering and passing away of all living beings, withdrew even from his companions, assumed the life of an ascetic and went in search of truth. After several years he abandoned extreme asceticism as a false path, and at length, while meditating beneath a tree, achieved supreme enlightenment. This involved a mental struggle with Māra, the evil one, the Lord of this world of passion, and the realization, through meditation and concentration, of the tranquillity and joy which come when all craving for permanence ceases. In this state of detachment he lost all pride and contempt for others, all self-intoxication. 'My mind was emancipated, ignorance was dispelled, knowledge

1

arose; darkness was dispelled, light arose.'

The story of the Buddha's enlightenment was greatly expanded in later tradition, but from it stem the basic teachings of early Buddhism, and especially the 'Four Supreme (or Noble) Truths': that life is suffering, that suffering is due to craving or desire, that this craving can be eliminated, and that there is a methodical way to such elimination. That way is the 'Supreme (or Noble) Eightfold Path', whose details need not concern us here, except to say that it too reflects the Buddha's own path to enlightenment and tranquillity through meditation and concentration.

Religious experience takes many different forms, and the religions of the world teach many different attitudes to the facts of suffering and evil. But it is not simply a matter of different practical and theoretical responses; the whole problem is seen differently in different religious contexts. We begin this study with the story of the Buddha's path to enlightenment, because early Buddhism stands at one extreme in the spectrum of religious attitudes to suffering, both in the way it sees the problem and in its response.

These two features are brought out very clearly in the story of the Buddha's encounters with the old man, the diseased man and the corpse, and the consequences of those encounters.

In the first place the stress is on suffering rather than on wickedness. What upsets Gautama's peace of mind is the fact of suffering, primarily physical suffering, although his own mental anguish is part of the problem too.

This distinction between physical and mental suffering on the one hand and human wickedness on the other needs to be clearly drawn, since the religions of the world differ in the stress they place on one or the other, both in diagnosis and in cure. Of course the two are related. On any view, human wickedness usually results in physical or mental suffering, not only for the victims of wickedness, but for the evil man himself, and on some views, wickedness is the cause of all suffering. This latter view, however, is hard to sustain. Most of us would admit that there is a great deal of suffering in the world which has nothing to do with human wickedness—senility, disease and death, for example. Nowadays, with our instant awareness through modern

2

communications systems of the extremity and extent of human suffering, we ourselves are constantly experiencing the mental anguish caused by encounter with the facts of suffering, with the results of natural disasters the world over: earthquakes, floods, famines and epidemics. We also know more these days about the harsher aspects of animal life and pain. So the problem of physical suffering looms large in our minds, just as it did in that of the Buddha.

Nevertheless, I suspect that we are equally aware of the problem of human wickedness, or radical moral evil: oppression, torture, ruthless aggression and pride in public life, cruelty and vicious selfishness in private life. We do not have to think only of Hitler's gas chambers. There is evidence enough all around us.

This distinction between human wickedness and physical and mental suffering is reflected in the title of this book: *Evil, Suffering and Religion*. Of course we do use the term 'evil' to cover both aspects, as when we talk of 'the problem of evil' in general. But when we distinguish between evil and suffering, as we do in our title, we tend to reserve 'evil' for wickedness, and 'suffering' for physical and mental suffering, whether caused by wickedness or not. Instead of 'suffering', we sometimes just speak of 'pain', and wrestle with 'the problem of pain'.

The two questions 'why are men often so wicked?' and 'why is there so much suffering in the world?' are certainly perplexing questions. They are different questions, but for us, I suspect, equally pressing ones.

The Buddha was clearly more perplexed by the second question than the first. It was the suffering (not only of men, but of all living beings) that caused his mental anguish in the first place, and became the main theme of his diagnosis of the human situation. It is true that in the struggle with the tempter, Māra, he had to overcome the lure of pride and discontent; and it is true that the Buddha came to believe that the cause of all suffering lay in craving or desire. But this is different from agonizing over human wickedness. To the Buddha the problem was the all-pervasiveness of physical and mental pain.

In the second place, the Buddha's response to suffering was much more a practical response, a way of coping with the facts,

3

than a theoretical attempt to explain or justify the presence of so much suffering in the world. When *we* ask 'why is there so much suffering in the world?', we tend to be looking for a reason, a purpose behind it all. Somehow things must make sense, or lead to something which makes it all worthwhile. But there is none of this in the Buddha's approach to the problem. Admittedly he offers one kind of explanation—a causal explanation in terms of universal craving; but that only pushes the question one stage further back: why are things like that? Why is there so much craving in the world? Why are men so ignorant of the truth, and why should the world be structured in such a way as to foster so much ignorance and suffering? Those questions did not interest the Buddha. Having diagnosed the source of suffering, he seeks only a practical way of curing the state in which men find themselves. Once you see the human predicament clearly, you need ask no further questions. A man gravely wounded by an arrow is interested only in the necessary surgery, not in where the arrow came from. You simply bring about the cessation of craving (at least in your own case) by spiritual techniques of meditation and concentration, until you reach a state of tranquillity beyond the reach of any suffering. This is not a self-centred reaction. For one thing it was part of Buddhist teaching that there is no permanent self, the illusory quest for self-identity being at the root of the whole problem. But also the Buddhist monks did not seek release only for themselves. Their mission was to teach others to find the way to enlightenment. The Buddha's compassion is one of the most attractive features of his religion. Later Buddhism developed the very moving doctrine of the Bodhisattvas, those who, on the verge of final and ultimate enlightenment, postpone their own release in order to help others on the way.

Even so, it is likely to strike the Westerner that to seek an ultimate detachment from the sufferings of the world, through an inner journey to enlightenment, has severe limitations as a complete answer to the problem of evil. Some of the aspects of the problem which are not adequately dealt with by early Buddhism are: the question of God; the question of human wickedness and the possibility of forgiveness; the ethical demands of inter-personal and social life; the question of human progress; the question of purpose or meaning in life. It is early Buddhism's lack of interest in these common religious questions that places it at one extreme in the spectrum of man's religious responses to the facts of suffering and evil.

IVAN KARAMAZOV

Let us turn to quite a different tradition and culture, and examine the story of Ivan Karamazov in Dostoevsky's novel, *The Brothers Karamazov*. There is a scene, which no one who has read the book can ever forget, in which Ivan visits his brother Alyosha in the monastery where Alyosha is a novice, and talks to him about his inability to accept God's world, because of the terrible wickedness and suffering it contains. He describes a number of instances of quite gratuitous cruelty and suffering— the mindless lashing of a worn-out horse by a drunken peasant, the pleasure taken by marauding Turks in blowing out a baby's brains in front of its mother, the case of a child who accidentally injured a Russian general's favourite hound, was stripped and made to run, and had the hounds set on him to tear him to pieces before his mother's eyes. 'I recognize in all humility' says Ivan, 'that I cannot understand why the world is arranged as it is.' He understands that men have been given freedom; but, he asks, is it worthwhile? Is God's purpose worth the tears of one tortured child? Even universal forgiveness and harmony in the future will not make it worth such sufferings. So he hastens to give back his entrance ticket. 'It's not God that I don't accept, Alyosha, only I most respectfully return Him the ticket.' And he clinches the argument by challenging his brother: 'Tell me yourself, I challenge you—answer. Imagine that you are creating a fabric of human destiny with the object of making men happy in the end, giving them peace and rest at last, but that it was essential and inevitable to torture to death only one tiny creature ... and to found that edifice on its unavenged tears, would you consent to be the architect on those conditions? Tell me, and tell the truth.'

'No I wouldn't consent,' said Alyosha softly ...

5

This conversation between the brothers captures vividly the terrible problem of both wickedness and suffering as it presents itself within the Christian tradition, with its highly developed belief in a creator God, who is, supposedly, the God of love. I admit that the extract from Dostoevsky is a very negative one. This conversation between Ivan and Alyosha does not attempt to give us an answer to or a way out of the problem of evil. But it does set out the problem as it appears to sensitive people brought up in the Christian tradition, and it indicates how differently the problem itself is seen and felt within the Christian tradition from the way in which it was seen and felt by the Buddha.

Two features in particular stand out sharply in what Ivan says. First, there is the emphasis on sheer human wickedness; the horror of these tales is the horror of boundless cruelty, deliberately indulged. It is not just a matter of the physical and mental suffering of the victims. That is bad enough, and Ivan sharpens his case by taking examples of the suffering of innocent children; but that suffering, in each case, is caused by wanton cruelty, and the outrage felt is at a universe in which such cruelty is permitted.

Secondly, it is belief in God that makes the problem so acute for Ivan. In the context of belief in a good creator God the presence of such cruelty and suffering in the world gives rise to a sense of moral outrage. Why does God permit it? This is primarily a problem for the understanding. 'I recognize in all humility that I cannot understand why the world is arranged as it is', says Ivan. The practical problem of coping with evil and suffering falls into the background. Dostoevsky believed that, as a problem for the understanding, there was no answer to the questions raised by Ivan Karamazov. The only thing that Christianity could set against the arguments of Ivan was the example of dedicated self-sacrificial love. That was what Dostoevsky hoped to show through the person of Alyosha. Not all Christians, however, have been so pessimistic about the theoretical problem. We shall be examining, along with the contributions of other religions, several Christian attempts to answer the problem of evil at the level of the understanding as well as at the practical level of self-sacrificial love.

The Judaeo-Christian, then, unlike the Buddhist tradition, sees the problem of evil first and foremost as involving a demand for explanation and justification. From the book of Job to Dostoevsky and to our own time the fundamental question has been, why does God allow all this evil and suffering? Why has God made a world in which such terrible things can and do take place? And even if we could show that the risk of things going wrong was an inevitable risk if God was to create a context of free personal life for his children, the question remains: was it worth it? Ivan's problem is a double one: he cannot understand why it was necessary for the world to be like this; and he cannot understand how it could be thought to be worth it—whatever the ultimate outcome.

The Judaeo-Christian tradition shares with the Buddhist tradition its horror at suffering—although one might well think that the horror is greatly sharpened when the suffering is seen as occurring in *God's* world—but it differs from the Buddhist tradition in singling out the cruelty and wickedness of man as being particularly horrifying. How can God's children be allowed to be so wicked?

SOME COMMENTS

From the vast literature of the world religions I have selected two stories to illustrate the themes which will be dealt with in this book. Already we have seen how different are the ways in which the problem of evil strikes the religious mind in different religious and cultural contexts, and how different are the responses encouraged and fostered within the different traditions. The two stories give rise to a number of general reflections.

In the first place, it is clear that the centrality of belief in God makes a big difference to how the problem strikes people. It is a remarkable feature of early Buddhism that it contains no belief in a supreme Being. One might think that for this reason alone early Buddhism hardly counts as a religion. On the other hand it has many other characteristic features of religion. It offers an all-embracing diagnosis of the human condition, and a

7

way out of the human predicament. It teaches meditative techniques for achieving ultimate release from self and suffering. Above all it holds there to be a final state of enlightenment and release which it calls Nirvāna and which it teaches men to think of as their ultimate concern. Furthermore, it organizes itself as a religion, with monks and missionaries and rituals. Any definition of religion which excluded early Buddhism would be too narrow. It should be thought of rather as the classical example of a non-theistic religion (that is, a religion without God).

The case of early Buddhism suggests the following general reflection: the less central belief in God is to a religion, the less will the problem of evil take the form of a demand for explanation. It will rather be a matter of correct diagnosis and the recommendation of a practical way out of the human predicament. Its emphasis will be on coping with the facts of evil. The understanding plays a part, obviously. One has to get the diagnosis right. One has to dispel the illusions of the King's palace where the young Gautama was at first kept shut in by his father. One has to face the facts. But once the facts are faced and the diagnosis made, the real emphasis lies on the best way to cope with and overcome the universal facts of suffering.

Conversely, if belief in God lies at the heart of a religion it will have to face the problem of evil, not only as something to be coped with, but as something to be explained. The problem becomes the more acute the more God is held to be both absolute in power and perfect in love. New ways of coping with evil and suffering may well come out of such a religion, but the main emphasis will lie on the need to understand.

Secondly, the less a religion is concerned with God, the more it is likely to concentrate on the problem of pain rather than that of human wickedness. This is perhaps a less obvious conclusion to draw, and I am certainly not claiming that it is proved by the two examples we have examined. After all it is not only the fact of belief in God that makes the difference. It also depends on what sort of God you believe in. It is because Christianity, like Judaism, has placed such stress on God as a righteous God that moral evil seems so problematic. Judaism and Christianity have certainly been instrumental in fostering the moral sense, and their sense of sin—to use the technical religious word—arises in direct relation to their sense of the righteousness and holiness of God. The more Christianity has emphasized the love of God, the more a sense of horror at human rebellion and human wickedness has come to characterize the Christian religious consciousness. Interestingly, this can work in opposite directions within the context of Christianity. The believer can be overwhelmed by the sense of his own sin and that of mankind; but equally the rebel's rejection of God's world can take the highly moral form of Ivan Karamazov's anguish at the facts of human cruelty in God's world. Buddhism, by contrast, does not have the same drive towards seeing this as, deep down, a moral problem.

These are some general reflections arising out of our two examples of the way in which the facts of suffering and evil can affect the religious consciousness of man. They suggest that we need to operate with two basic distinctions: first, the distinction between the problem of pain (suffering) and the problem of wickedness (evil); secondly, the distinction between coping with these things and explaining or understanding their presence in the world.

THE PLAN OF THIS BOOK

The plan of this book follows our recognition of these basic distinctions. We concentrate first on the problem of coping with suffering and evil. Putting on one side the question of explanation, we shall survey the religions of the world for the practical resources they offer men for meeting and dealing with both aspects of this darker side of human life and experience, with physical and mental suffering, and with moral evil.

Then we shall turn to the other, more theoretical problem. We shall survey the religions of the world for the beliefs they teach about the origin of evil and why it is such a common feature of human experience. Since, as we have already noted, this problem looms larger in religions where belief in God is central, we shall from then on be concentrating on the theistic religions. The reason why much more space is going to be given to the

9

theoretical problem of explaining evil than to the practical problem of coping with it is that books are, by and large, the place for exploring theories and beliefs. If one has a difficulty in understanding or justifying some belief, then the natural thing to do is to read about it and think it through with the help of other people's ideas. Now the world religions include whole developing traditions of belief and understanding, and one has to study them in detail and in depth, if one is ever going to grasp the possibilities of explanation that they offer. But the practical problem of coping with suffering and evil will never be solved by reading books and thinking. One has actually to meet religious people, Buddhists, Hindus, Christians, Jews, Muslims, and see how they in fact confront the world's evil, if one is going to grasp something of the resources of religion for coping with suffering and wrong. A certain amount can be learned from books, especially from biographical accounts, like that of the Buddha's own enlightenment. But talking to a Buddhist and living in a Buddhist community are far better ways of studying the practical aspects of our problem.

Concentrating, then, on the theoretical problems and on the theistic religions where the theoretical problems are most pressing, we shall proceed to look at the problem of moral evil, and at the argument one often meets in the literature of religion, that the gift of free will, without which persons would not exist, explains why God allows men to choose the evil as well as the good.

Then we shall turn back to the problem of suffering and ask in more detail why the physical world is so arranged and structured that pain and suffering are inevitable consequences for sentient, conscious beings such as man.

On the basis of our reflections and discoveries in these chapters we shall go on to ask the question whether any of the world religions has succeeded in developing a credible understanding of divine providence, that is to say, of the way God cares for the world and fulfils his purpose in and through it.

Finally we shall try to bring together the themes of coping with evil and explaining evil by surveying the different ways in which the religions of the world have envisaged the ultimate

10

overcoming of evil and suffering. This is the place where we shall look at the religions' hopes and beliefs about the future.

Such is the plan for the main part of this book. But there will be at the end an appendix about animals. The Buddha, we recall, was appalled at the suffering of all living things, not just that of men and women; Ivan Karamazov told the harrowing story of the mindless lashing of a worn-out horse; and the problem of animal pain has often been presented as a special problem for a religion such as Christianity, which has taught that every sparrow is the object of God's care.

SOME SOCIOLOGICAL CONSIDERATIONS

The bulk of this book presupposes that the problem of evil is a real problem, and that the religions, in their different ways, have something worthwhile to say about it. But that presupposition has itself to be examined in Religious Studies, and we have to reckon with alternative accounts of what is going on in the attempts of the religions to grapple with the problem of evil, both practically and theoretically. Sociological accounts are particularly important in this respect, for on any view, whatever the truth or falsity of religious beliefs, membership of a close-knit religious group is a solace and resource against the blows of ill-fortune and against the threat of meaninglessness. One of the strengths of Buddhism has always been the Sangha, the community of Buddhist monks, and the appeal of monastic communities in Christianity is in part to be explained by the proven ability of such ordered groups to provide men and women with mutual reinforcement in the practice of religious discipline. Sociologists are interested in the way such community life supports the individual in a hostile environment. Similarly they are interested in the way in which membership of a close-knit sectarian community can give a strong focus of meaning and encouragement to the bewildered and the broken. A clear example of such social forces at work can be seen in the rise of new religions in Japan since the end of the Second World War. At a time of unparalleled national disaster and suffering these groups, often nationalistic as well as religious, provided a context

11

of meaning and mutual support for their members. The same is true in varying degrees of any religious group, and indeed of the dedicated Marxist cell.

Nevertheless, the religions of the world do not only provide the resources of group commitment and community life against the tribulations of human existence; they also claim to offer true diagnoses of the human condition, and appropriate ways of understanding and coping with evil, ways which correspond with how things actually are. So while we accept the relevance of sociological study at the level of the practical effects on the individual of group membership, we shall be more concerned here with people's beliefs about reality and the resources which they believe to be actually available to them.

However, it is possible to study religious beliefs as well as religious communities from a sociological point of view. The sociologist can investigate the whole system of belief fostered and developed by a particular religion simply as a human construct, a world of meaning projected out on to the universe. To do the job of providing a context of ultimate meaning, the sociologist can argue, a religion has to retain its plausibility in the face of experience; and so he can treat the efforts of religious thinkers to solve the problem of evil as no more than the struggle to retain consistency in their systems of belief, whether or not their beliefs are true. An interesting example of such an approach to the question of theodicy (justifying the ways of God to man) is to be found in a book entitled *The Social Reality of Religion* by Peter Berger (Penguin). He argues there that it is the break-down in its 'plausibility structure' in the face of the horrors of twentieth-century war and the Nazi atrocities that has caused Christianity to lose its hold on the western mind. The deliberate presupposition of Berger's discussion is that he refrains from asking questions about the truth or falsity of religious views. All he is interested in (in this book) is the consistency of a set of ideas in the face of human experience.

We too shall be interested in the consistency of the systems of belief included in the world religions. But we shall be study-ing them as different beliefs about reality. The Buddha un-doubtedly taught the Four Noble Truths as *truths*, a diagnosis of

12

how things actually are. Similarly Ivan Karamazov was not concerned about the consistency of a set of ideas which Christians project upon the universe. He was genuinely angry with the Christian God. This book is undertaken in the conviction that the way to do Religious Studies is not to ignore the truth claims of religion, but to put oneself in the shoes of believers of many traditions and try to see how reality appears to each of them. We are comparing, that is to say, different truth claims, some of which may actually turn out to be true.

2

COPING WITH EVIL AND SUFFERING

In this chapter we concentrate on practical approaches. We postpone examination of the 'why' questions which people ask when confronted by the facts of evil, and focus our attention on the different ways which different religions recommend of coping with the facts of evil. This is not to ignore people's beliefs. Beliefs about the world shape men's practical responses, for they determine how men see the problem of suffering. But our emphasis is on what they consider the most appropriate way of doing something about it.

First, however, by way of contrast, let us look at some non-religious ways of coping with evil; for the unbeliever, too, is unavoidably faced with evil and suffering and has to fashion some kind of practical response. We take one example from the ancient world and two from the modern world.

NON-RELIGIOUS WAYS OF COPING WITH EVIL

The Roman poet and philosopher Lucretius, who lived in the first century B.C., wrote a long poem, *On the Nature of Things*, in order to free men from religious fears. Lucretius was a follower of the Greek philosopher Epicurus, Epicureanism being one of the major materialist philosophies in the ancient world. For Lucretius religion and the fears it induced were part of the world's evil, and to reject religion altogether was a major step towards peace of mind. Of course Lucretius, just as anyone else, had to find some way of coping with physical suffering and human wickedness. His answer, like that of his master Epicurus, was the contemplation, as far as possible, of lasting pleasure and tranquillity of mind. Believing that the world and man himself

14

are nothing but a chance concourse of atoms, the wise man, according to Lucretius, sets himself austerely to pursue the goals of truth, peace and happiness. Epicureanism is not, as it is sometimes presented, the selfish and undisciplined pursuit of pleasure; rather, it is the fearless and calm quest for those virtues which alone bring lasting happiness in a world such as this. Free from superstition, remorse and passion, the wise man simply cultivates friendship and knowledge, putting away all sources of mental suffering.

It is interesting to compare this non-religious quest for tranquillity with that of the early Buddhism which we were discussing in chapter one. Clearly Lucretius and the Epicureans remain much more on the surface of things. Their philosophical calm is less arduously achieved, and it might seem to be more a matter of temperament than the result of a profound struggle to place oneself outside the range of fate or fortune. The Buddha's hard-won mystical state of enlightenment is something very different from Lucretius' concentration on the pursuit of truth and peace of mind. Nevertheless both are aware of the evils of craving and passion, both wish to be free from unnecessary beliefs and fears, and both seek for themselves and their fellows a way of escape from the influence of the world's ills.

If Lucretius and the Epicureans strike us as lacking in profundity in their response to the problem of evil, let us turn to the modern atheistic French writer, Albert Camus (1913–60), for a more profound grappling with evil. In his novel, *The Plague*, Camus describes the reactions of a number of characters to the terrible plague which devastates the town of Oran. The plague is not only an example of the physical suffering which afflicts mankind, it also explicitly symbolizes the corrupting evils which attack men from within. (It has also been taken to symbolize the social and political evil of the Nazi occupation of France.) Camus' own response seems to be identified with that of the atheist Dr Rieux, who works night and day to relieve the suffering. Rieux, with his profoundly felt rejection of religious consolation, seems to be fashioning, in the face of evil, not just an atheistic humanism, but a kind of atheistic sanctity. He asks his friend explicitly: 'Can one be a saint without God? That's

15

the problem, in fact, the only problem I'm up against today'. Rieux exemplifies, not only in his work to relieve suffering but also in his personal attitudes, the kind of human integrity in the face of appalling suffering that makes one speak of sainthood.

There is no doubt that the possibility of such a stance against the facts of evil is a remarkable and profound human fact, and it makes the Epicurean's philosophy of calm seem very shallow by comparison. But can Camus' ideal of atheistic sanctity ever be expected to contain the resources to help the countless millions of ordinary human sufferers? For all its admirable qualities, is it not too cultured, too intellectual, to be more than an inspiration for the few?

For a second example from the modern world we turn to Marxism, undoubtedly one of the most powerful social and political movements ever to appear upon the human scene. Marx began his critique of existing society with an attack on religion for providing a false way of reconciling men to their present suffering. Only when they came to realize the material and economic forces underlying different forms of social order, could they see how these might actually be changed and an equal and just society created in which many of the ills that have beset mankind would be overcome. Marxism, therefore, sets up the goal of a future classless society, for which men now can struggle and the realization of which will make their present sufferings worthwhile. In other words the practical answer of Marxism to the facts of evil is to struggle to overcome those social ills that can, according to its theory, be overcome. It has nothing to say about those evils which, on any mundane view, can never be overcome—natural disasters, old age and death, for example. Marxism does claim to be able to overcome the evils of human wickedness, since crime will allegedly disappear when everyone is co-operating in the classless society. Some evidence to support this analysis of human nature has been cited, particularly from China; but it could well be argued that the totalitarian nature of existing Marxist societies has on the contrary added greatly to the sum of human evil.

It is interesting to observe that these three non-religious

responses to the facts of evil (that of Lucretius in the ancient world, and those of Camus and the Marxists in the modern world) all involve a radical critique and rejection of religion. Man is held to be alone in the universe and must use his own resources to cope with evil and suffering. But these three responses are very different in kind. One, that of Lucretius, represents a resigned quest for wisdom and peace: a man should try to make himself and encourage others to be as little vulnerable as possible to the world's ills. The second, that of Camus, is heroic and activist in its struggle to relieve suffering. It is individualistic in its quest for integrity, and also fundamentally pessimistic in its picture of what can be done. The third, that of the Marxists, is much more optimistic and less individualistic. Marxists bring to their determination to change the conditions of society the dedication and the power of a close-knit group, the Party.

We shall see these different kinds of response to the facts of evil recurring in religious contexts, along with the specifically religious ways of coping.

RELIGIOUS WAYS OF COPING WITH EVIL

In turning to religious practical responses to evil, we enter upon an enormous field, comprising the larger part of the history of the human race. There seems to be no human society, however far back we go into pre-history, and however far we range among surviving non-literate tribes in the world today, which was or is totally without some recognizably religious response to the world.

TRIBAL RELIGIONS

As we look at the tribal religions of Asia, Africa, South America or Australasia, taking them as clues to man's religious past, we are liable at first to feel the force of Lucretius' and the Marxists' view that religion has actually added to the problem rather than diminished it. For the world of tribal religion appears at first sight to be a world of magic and sorcery and, at best, divine

17

reward and punishment, which greatly increase the felt experience of evil, whether natural or human. The harm that men can do each other seems to be greatly enlarged where it is believed that mystical powers or curses can affect a man's crops, his animals or his family. Natural disasters seem even more devastating if they are believed to be either the result of some malicious will or evidence of divine displeasure. Professor John Mbiti, writing on *African Religions and Philosophy* (Heinemann), says that one has to grow up in an African village to get an idea of the depth of evil experienced and felt by members of a close-knit tribal society.

But there is another side to the picture. It is not just that tribal religions also provide remedies for the ills that afflict individuals and the tribe, remedies such as rituals, medicine-men, sacrifices and the like, which are believed to counter the alleged malicious use of power by the living or the dead. It is also important to realize that such frameworks of belief have the function of making everything that happens intelligible to the people whose whole life and experience fall within those frameworks. Furthermore, tribal religions are not just a matter of magic and priestcraft. To a surprising extent, especially in Africa, anthropologists have discovered that they include belief in a supreme Being who cares for social morality and punishes infringements and crimes. Even the rituals and spells have more than functional significance. They do not only encourage men to think that they have the ability to ward off the blows of fate; they also contribute to a personalized view of the world, where life is felt and experienced as ultimately meaningful. Coming from a scientific culture, we tend to disparage these as primitive prescientific beliefs, and for a long time anthropologists thought that tribal religion showed up the illusory origins of all religious responses to the world. But the argument can work the other way. Granted that, anthropologically speaking, the so-called higher religions have their origins in non-literate tribal religion, nevertheless the world religions in the course of time have discovered that the spiritual dimension of life and its resources for living in the face of the world's evils are not necessarily bound up with prescientific belief. Tribal religions may have mistaken the

18

relation between spiritual resources and scientific causation; but the very possibility of a religion which does not confuse the spiritual with the scientific shows that the tribal religions' experience of God is not necessarily pure illusion. The student of religion has to consider the possibility that, for all its distortion in superstition, witchcraft and magic, tribal religion has glimpsed the fact that man is not alone in the universe and that there are spiritual resources available to help men cope with evil.

It is the discernment of the possibility of spiritual resources in a world of pain and wickedness that marks out a specifically religious response to evil. At the primitive level which we are discussing here, these resources tend to be thought of as powers to be propitiated, cajoled into providing help or even manipulated; but they also provide sanctions against wrong-doing and a source of spiritual succour in times of need or temptation.

THE RELIGIONS OF GREECE AND ROME

A very different picture is presented by the complex literary culture of the classical world. In fact, the Greek gods Zeus and Hera, Artemis, Ares and Poseidon (or their Roman equivalents Jupiter and Juno, Diana, Mars and Neptune) were probably less satisfactory as resources against evil than the tribal gods, just because of the highly developed literary mythologies. Although these gods took their origin in the sense of divine power in the great forces of nature, sky and earth, sun and moon and sea, the Homeric stories, learned by every child at school, may well have prevented the growth within the official religion of more ethical responses or a deeper kind of monotheism. Certainly the rituals of sacrifice and the consultation of oracles played much the same role in the classical world as they did in tribal religion; even Socrates gave instructions to his friends to sacrifice a cock to Asclepius just before he died. But it is clear that the polytheistic mythologies failed to meet men's deeper religious needs. Thus for an ethical response men turned to philosophy, whether that of Socrates, Plato or Aristotle or that of the Epicureans, whom we have already mentioned (pp. 14f).

Another and more religious philosophical position in the

19

classical world was that of Stoicism—a movement going back to Zeno (c. 300 B.C.) but embraced by several leading Romans, including the emperor Marcus Aurelius (A.D. 121–180). The Stoics believed that the universe has a divinely given rational order with which men ought to live in harmony. All men have a divine spark within them. Indeed the Stoic belief in the all-pervasive divine Logos (rational power) has led to their being thought of as pantheists. Much of their thought, moreover, has a determinist ring about it. Since the whole world is providentially ordered, men should resign themselves to whatever losses they suffer. Stoic apathy (or resignation) has become the characteristic by which their philosophy of life has been remembered. As is the case with all summary phrases, 'Stoic apathy' fails to capture the subtlety of a complex system of thought, especially in its emphasis on wisdom and the virtues. But Stoicism certainly represents a religious form of that resigned approach to the world's ills which we have already singled out as one characteristic human response.

The popular mind, however, looked elsewhere for religious satisfaction and religious consolation. The popularity of the mystery religions, spreading westwards from the near east, the frenzied cult of Dionysus, or the secret rites associated with the saviour god Mithras, indicate the need of something more personal and esoteric. Men found release, 'salvation', through the religious enthusiasm which these close-knit groups engendered. Here too we encounter a characteristic religious response to the world's ills. Men are taken out of themselves and their problems in the experience of religious ecstasy.

But opposite tendencies were also evident at the popular level in the ancient world—the tendency to worship chance or destiny, for example, or, in Rome, to worship the political order represented by the semi-divine figure of the emperor. If men's lives are really controlled by chance, or if they really depend for their security on the powerful structure of the empire, then these forces themselves become the object of religious devotion. Thus one way of responding to what determines men's fate is to make that very thing the focus of a cult. One can think of these tendencies as reflecting at the popular level the same kind of religious response as Stoicism represented at a more intellectual philosophical level.

THE LIVING RELIGIONS OF THE WORLD

Our survey now broadens out to examine characteristic ways of coping with evil taught in the major religions of the world, east and west. The majority of our examples will be taken from Hinduism, Buddhism, Judaism, Christianity and Islam, but from time-to-time we shall need to look at the other religions of Persia, India, China and Japan.

Five ways of meeting evil will be distinguished: the way of renunciation, the way of mystical knowledge, the way of devotion, the way of works and the way of sacrifice.

THE WAY OF RENUNCIATION

It is a remarkable fact that, throughout the history of religions, more pervasively in the east than in the west, but at times in every religious tradition, asceticism has been manifested as a powerful religious ideal and as a way of confronting the world's evil. An ascetic is one who by renunciation and self-discipline, sometimes to the point of self torture, seeks to free himself from all bodily attachments. As this definition suggests, the path of asceticism is seldom undertaken for its own sake, but rather in conjunction with a negative evaluation of the physical world and in the interests of a positive religious ideal, whether of knowledge, devotion, or sacrifice. Consequently this first way of meeting evil cannot be isolated from the others.

The wandering ascetic is a notable figure in Hinduism, the dominant religion of India and the oldest of the world's living religions. In the Hindu tradition, after a man had been educated, and had performed his duty as a householder, ideally he freed himself from all bonds and went off into the forest to lead the life of a hermit, and eventually that of a wandering ascetic. This austere ideal cannot be understood until one has grasped the nature of the Indian quest for liberation or release (*moksha*). It is a fundamental belief of almost all forms of Indian religion

21

that life is an endless round of birth and rebirth, a constant cycle of reincarnation, in which each man's place is determined by the consequences of his action in previous lives. On this view, evil and suffering are to be coped with at two different levels. At one level a man should try to live rightly in accordance with the moral order (*dharma*), so that he may earn a better place in his next incarnation. But at another level he should seek to escape from the whole cycle of rebirth, so that he is no longer caught in its endless toils. This is the goal of ultimate release. It is this goal that inspires the ascetic life.

Hinduism has envisaged the path to such release in several different ways. The classical Hindu treatises known as the Upanishads teach mainly a way of mystical knowledge. The Bhagavad Gītā, a later extremely popular scripture, puts the way of devotion to the Lord Krishna above the way of knowledge. But in both cases, techniques of self-discipline and meditation, known throughout the Indian tradition as *yoga*, are taught not for their own sake but as means of acquiring mystical or devotional release. The Bhagavad Gītā, indeed, frowns on extreme asceticism and teaches the art of detachment while fully engaged in one's active duties.

More extreme forms of asceticism are to be found in Jainism. The Jains are the followers of the Jinas ('victorious ones'), ancient sages who taught the way of salvation. Mahāvīra, probably a contemporary of the Buddha (sixth century B.C.) is the best known of these and his teachings are the main focus of Jainism, which, like Buddhism, presupposes much of the common Indian heritage, but in its reaction against the Hindu system of caste and sacrifice became a separate religion rather than an unorthodox sect. In Jainism the path to release is an arduous one of extreme renunciation and asceticism. The Jain monk practises self-mortification and deep meditation, and goes to extraordinary lengths to avoid injuring any living being. He wears a gauze mask to prevent breathing in insects and sweeps the ground in front of him to avoid crushing any creature.

Buddhism, too, involves renunciation, as we saw in chapter 1 in the story of the Buddha's path to enlightenment. Suffering no longer overwhelms the man who has renounced all craving and

22

desire. The Buddha himself abandoned extreme asceticism after trying it for some years. This was one of the ways in which he rejected the characteristic Hindu ideals of his time. Nevertheless, the many-sided developments of Buddhism have included the growth of ascetic sects, for instance, in Tibet.

Asceticism is uncharacteristic of the far east, but we do find it taught in one of the rivals to Confucianism in the so-called 'age of the philosophers' in ancient China. Confucius himself taught more of an ethical philosophy of life than a specifically religious way, but Mo Tzu (c. 400 B.C.) advocated extreme asceticism as a form of self-sacrifice on all men's behalf. Thus in the Chinese context we see the way of renunciation being held up as an ideal in conjunction with the way of sacrifice rather than with the way of mystical knowledge or the way of devotion.

Retracing our steps westward we find in the middle east a distinctive form of ethical monotheism based on the conviction of God's revelation of himself in history to the chosen people Israel. The problem of evil came to be sharply felt in Judaism and in its daughter religion, Christianity, but it was seldom confronted by the kind of ascetic response which we are at present examining. The way of renunciation has its place in Judaism and Christianity, but largely in the context of repentance for wrong-doing and discipline for the service of God and man, not of wholesale rejection of the world. But there have been moments in the history of Judaism and Christianity when asceticism has been strongly advocated in the quest for perfection. Thus the Essenes, a Jewish sect at the time of Jesus, cut themselves off from ordinary social institutions and formed an ascetic community, awaiting the coming of the Messiah, God's agent in bringing history to a close and ushering in God's reign.

More extreme forms of asceticism emerged in the context of Christianity in the third century A.D., when hermits such as St Anthony set up their cells in the deserts of Egypt. The idea of withdrawal from the world in the interests of Christian perfection was soon regulated and controlled by the institution of the monastic orders in Christianity, which continue to inspire many Christian men and women today as a form of unconditional self-dedication. But even where renunciation has taken heroic

23

forms, it has either been primarily for the sake of one's fellows, as with St Francis, or in the interests of mystical knowledge, as with St John of the Cross in Spain. The most ascetic monastic order in Christendom is the Carthusian order of contemplative monks, who renounce the world in order to devote themselves to God. It is a remarkable feature of Christian asceticism, as opposed to that of the east, that it does not prevent the expression of a great love for the created world, as in the poems of St Francis.

The way in which asceticism tends to go with the search for mystical union with God is illustrated by the growth of Sufi mysticism in Islam. In its dominant form the Muslim faith, the religion of the followers of Muhammad (c. A.D. 570–632), is non-mystical and non-ascetic, being rather a religion of law and devotion. But already by the eighth century ascetic movements had found a place within the Muslim fold, as a means to the mystical vision of God. Muslim mysticism is known as Sufism from the word for undyed wool (*suf*), which the ascetics wore.

Asceticism is an ambiguous phenomenon in the history of religions, and its extreme forms have often been condemned, not only in the religions which see the world as God's good creation. Renunciation does not necessarily involve disparagement of the world, but it has taken its more extreme forms where the material world is believed to be illusion or even evil. Of course if matter is evil, then the only valid response is to seek to free the soul from its entanglement in matter by the practice of asceticism. This was the view of the Manichees in third century Persia, whose dualist solution to the problem of evil will be discussed in the next chapter.

In the modern western world the way of renunciation has lost much of its appeal, partly through the discovery of successful means of improving man's material condition, and partly through an increased sense of responsibility for the world. But it has a persistent attraction for many religious minds in face of the manifest injustices in the distribution of the world's goods.

24

Whether accompanied by asceticism or not, the quest for mystical knowledge has been one of the major religious responses to the world's evil. It can take a number of forms: some people have found in nature-mysticism a solace from all that causes pain. A sense of oneness with nature, as powerfully evoked in Wordsworth's poems, for example, can take a man out of himself into communion with

> A presence that disturbs me with the joy
> Of elevated thought; a sense sublime
> Of something far more deeply interfused,
> Whose dwelling is the light of setting suns,
> And the round ocean and the living air,
> And the blue sky, and in the mind of man:
> A motion and a spirit, that impels
> All thinking things, all objects of all thought,
> And rolls through all things.[1]

This identification of all things, including ourselves, with the divine spirit is known as pantheism.

In other contexts of belief mysticism is held to involve the union of the soul with some transcendent power or spirit behind or beyond the veil of the natural world. This can take impersonal or personal forms. But similar experiences can be quite differently interpreted as simply the isolation of the soul or self in a state beyond the reach of change or chance or suffering. Consequently mystical experience is not confined to systems of pantheistic or theistic belief.

It is difficult to describe the way of mystical knowledge, because words are held to be inadequate to do it justice. Teachers of mysticism always claim that it can be understood only by treading the mystical path itself.

Indian religion has fostered and taught the way of mystical knowledge as one of the chief ways to ultimate release from the round of rebirth. In Hinduism this tradition is summed up in the

---

[1] *Lines composed a few miles above Tintern Abbey.* ll. 83–91.

25

Upanishads, philosophical and mystical treatises dating from about 800 B.C. onwards, in which is taught the ultimate identity of Ātman, the soul, and Brahman, the supreme and all-pervasive power of the universe. Such knowledge is to be acquired through renunciation, spiritual exercises and instruction by a teacher or guru.

While such knowledge is held to lead to ultimate release from the round of rebirth, it is also seen as a possibility for men still engaged in the duties of life. Thus in the Bhagavad Gītā Krishna, an incarnation of the god Vishnu, speaks of the wise who 'while yet in this world ... have overcome the process of emanation and decay, for their minds are stilled in that-which-is-ever-the-same ...'[2]

In later Hinduism there developed several schools of philosophy, of which one in particular, known as Advaita (non-dualist) Vedānta, sums up the teaching of the Upanishads on the identity of Ātman and Brahman and treats it as the essence of Hinduism. The most uncompromising exponent of this school was the philosopher-saint Shankara (A.D. 788–820), who taught that Brahman alone is real. The world is illusion and freedom from it comes with the realization of the soul's identity with Brahman. In Shankara's teaching the absolute reality, insofar as it can be described at all, is called Being, Consciousness and Bliss.

It should be noted that the kind of absolute monism exemplified in Shankara's teaching involves the view that evil and suffering are themselves illusory. This kind of mysticism, then, escapes the world's ills by coming to recognize them as ultimately unreal.

The view that suffering is illusion is clearly an extreme position to adopt. So is the view that the self which suffers is ultimately unreal. We find this other extreme asserted in Buddhism. We have already seen how the Buddha's quest for mystical enlightenment did not involve belief in God or in a metaphysical Absolute. He taught rather a way of meditation and concentration that itself brought about release. This comes about through the realization that there is no such thing as the

[2] *Bhagavad Gītā*, ed., R. C. Zaehner (O.U.P.) 5.19.

self. In realizing this one escapes the toils of craving or desire and attains the ultimate goal of Nirvāna. Nirvāna is described in Buddhist literature largely in negative terms, again because no words can do it justice. It is illustrated by such models as the extinction of a candle flame. Nevertheless, it cannot be thought of as nothing at all. Experientially speaking, Nirvāna seems to be envisaged as a timeless mystical state, and metaphysically speaking, as a transcendent state, beyond the reach of all human categories.

Another example of the way of mystical knowledge, more reminiscent of Hinduism than of Buddhism, is the ancient Chinese religion of Taoism (*tao* means 'way'). Its classical scripture is the *Tao Te Ching* ('the Way and its Power'), attributed to Lao Tzu (sixth century B.C.), but probably much later. Its doctrine is that there is an inexpressible divine principle behind the universe, with which the wise man seeks to reach harmony. By stilling the sense and emptying the mind the mystic reaches an inner perception of and unity with the eternal Tao. It is interesting to observe that Taoism did not require ascetic methods. It was a passive and quietist type of mysticism, involving profound awareness of the peace and beauty of nature.

In the course of time, under the influence of Mahāyāna Buddhism (the later form of Buddhism which spread through China and Japan in the second and sixth centuries A.D. respectively) Taoism developed a more complicated mythology and cult and itself contributed to the growth of Zen Buddhism in Japan.

Zen Buddhism rejects arduous methods of achieving illumination. It teaches, rather, calm and harmonious practices in everyday life, such as the tea ceremony, and meditation on a form of words, the *koan*, given to each pupil by the Zen master. Protracted meditation on this, whether in the hall of meditation in the Zen temple, or while ploughing in the field, is held to lead spontaneously to the mystical experience.

Western mysticism has usually taken the personal form of an ecstatically felt union with God or Christ or Allāh. As we have already seen, it has often been held to involve ascetic practices and renunciation of the world, but not the belief that the world is evil or illusory. In the history of both Christianity and Islam

27

mystics have been suspected of heresy and have sometimes been persecuted, usually for exaggerated claims of identity with God. Thus the Muslim Sufi mystic, Al Hallāj, was crucified in A.D. 922 for claiming 'I am the Real'. But western mystics, too, have from time to time expressed their sense of mystical union in more impersonal language reminiscent of the East. Thus there are elements in the teaching of the fourteenth-century German mystic, Meister Eckhart, which point away from traditional Christian theism to a sense of union with a supreme reality beyond personality.

More typical of Christian mysticism are these two quotations, one from St Teresa of Avila (A.D. 1515–82), the other from St John of the Cross (A.D. 1542–91):

> While seeking God in this way, the soul is conscious that it is fainting almost completely away in a kind of swoon, with a very great calm and joy. Its breath and all its bodily powers progressively fail it ... The whole physical strength vanishes ... and the strength of the soul increases for the better enjoyment of its bliss ... Then the Lord said to me: 'It dissolves utterly, my daughter, to rest more and more in Me. It is no longer itself that lives, it is I.'

> In this tranquillity the understanding sees itself raised up in a new and strange way, above all natural understanding, to the Divine light, much as one who, after a long sleep, opens his eyes to the light which he was not expecting.

As we reflect on the various forms of mystical experience cultivated and recommended in the religions of the world, we can certainly see how these exalted forms of consciousness might well be thought to lift men up beyond the reach of many of the world's ills. The phenomenon of mystical experience is indeed so widespread and recurrent that many students of religion have concluded that it is the essence of religion and religion's chief resource for suffering humanity. On the other hand it has been questioned whether it is really a resource available to all, or whether it requires a special temperament or vocation. Mysticism, if cultivated for its own sake, can appear to be a self-indulgent and anti-social phenomenon, although the religions vary in the degrees to which they permit the pursuit of mystical knowledge to the neglect of one's fellows. Both Buddhism and Christianity have strongly discouraged any movement which neglects the practice of compassion and love; and the strength and inspiration for self-sacrificial living have been claimed to come from mystical experience itself. Hinduism, in some of its many forms, has been criticized for teaching the possibility of ultimate detachment even from ethical concern. A further question is raised by the fact that many of the states described in the literature of mysticism can apparently be simulated by the use of drugs.

THE WAY OF DEVOTION

The Bhagavad Gītā, despite its recognition of the way of mystical knowledge, in fact places the way of devotion (*bhakti*) to the Lord Krishna on a higher plane. This reflects the growth within Hinduism of popular devotional cults in reaction against the abstruse mystical philosophy of the Upanishads. In so far as religion helps the ordinary Hindu to cope with the facts of evil and suffering, it is primarily through the temple cults of the supreme gods Vishnu or Shiva, or the mother goddess, Devī, or the many lesser divinities whose shrines and ceremonies are a central part of Indian village life. Philosophical Hindus may see these gods as manifestations at a lower level of the supreme Brahman, but to the popular mind they are themselves the principal religious reality with which men have to do. One has only to think of the vast pilgrimages to the Ganges, or the Jagannāth festival at Purī, when the figure of the god is taken out to his summer residence on a huge cart, to realize that the felt resources of religion for the majority of Indians are the resources of devotional enthusiasm.

The Bhagavad Gītā sees devotion to the Lord Krishna as performing precisely the same function of releasing men from the round of rebirth as the more arduous way of mystical knowledge. Thus Krishna says:

But those who cast off all their works on Me, solely intent
29

on Me, and meditate on Me in spiritual exercise, leaving no room for others, and so really do Me know, these will I lift up on high out of the ocean of recurring death, and that right soon, for their thoughts are fixed on me.[3]

The reference to meditation on Krishna by spiritual exercise shows that the mystical tradition is still affecting the way in which devotion to the god is understood, even when priority is given to devotion.

A notable feature of Hindu devotional theism is the belief in divine incarnations known as Avatārs ('descents'). Krishna in the Bhagavad Gīta is an incarnation of the god Vishnu, and the Avatār doctrine is summed up in these verses:

... whenever the law of righteousness withers away and lawlessness arises, then do I generate myself on earth. For the protection of the good, for the destruction of evildoers, for the setting up of the law of righteousness I come into being age after age.[4]

Hindu mythology contains many Avatārs, and modern Hindus will even speak of the Buddha, Jesus Christ and Gandhi as Avatārs, bringing the divine help when things have gone particularly wrong. The Avatār, especially Krishna, is the focus of a widespread cult and is the source of great religious power and solace for his devotees.

The same pressure to provide a devotional focus for the religious heart and mind is to be found in the developments of Buddhism, despite the Buddha's lack of interest in the gods. In Mahāyāna Buddhism cults of devotion to Buddhas and Bodhisattvas (Buddhas-to-be) became widespread; they appear as semi-divine figures, celestial Buddhas, faith in whom can bring enlightenment to those unable to acquire it for themselves. In the Pure Land, or Lotus, school of Chinese and Japanese Buddhism such enlightenment was thought of as rebirth in the Pure Land of the West (the Buddhist paradise). In its Japanese

[3] *Bhagavad Gītā*, ed., R. C. Zaehner (O.U.P.) 12.6–7.
[4] Op. cit., 4.7–8.

form this school developed a remarkable theology of grace. The Buddha Amida became an object of worship, able to transfer his infinite merit to those who have faith in him.

In the sixteenth century A.D. a pure form of devotional monotheism was developed by the Sikhs in the north-west Indian state of the Punjab. The Sikhs are followers of Guru Nanak (A.D. 1469–1439), who taught that the only way of salvation from illusory worldly values is a disciplined growing into union with 'the one God, the creator, omnipresent, immortal'.

Sikhism shares with Judaism, Christianity and Islam a more austere moral element than is to be found in most eastern devotional religion. Judaism was the earliest religion to develop so powerful a sense of the holiness and righteousness of God. The consequence of this is a greater emphasis on human sin and the need for repentance, if individuals or the nation are to receive divine succour. Yet the availability of divine succour is undoubtedly the principal theme of devotional religion in the western theistic tradition. One has only to read the Psalms in the Hebrew Bible to capture the sense of the resources of devotional religion in face of suffering and human wickedness. Similarly today, despite all the suffering of the Jewish people in our own time, and despite the unparalleled human wickedness to which they have been subjected, orthodox Jews look to God to vindicate his people, and see the setting up of the state of Israel as one more indication of the way in which God brings his people out of exile into the promised land.

Christianity draws much of its power to enable men and women to cope with the world's evil from its central focus, the Cross of Christ. As is the case with Judaism and Islam, Christianity has much to say about repentance, atonement and forgiveness; but its distinctive belief and resource over against evil and suffering is its conviction that God has himself, without ceasing to be God, entered into the depths of human suffering and taken it upon himself. Thus Christian devotion is devotion to Christ crucified, and the strength Christianity claims to provide for coping with evil is drawn from communion with the one whom the philosopher A. N. Whitehead (A.D. 1861–1947) called 'the fellow-sufferer who understands'. Christians have been taught to regard this communion as sometimes involving a share in the sufferings of Christ. By such spiritual identification they are held to be enabled to bear pain and suffering creatively.

The word *islam* means 'submission', and it is belief in the one sovereign God, Allāh, who controls the world and men, and to whom men should submit themselves in devotion and duty, that gives Islam its characteristic form. The simplicity and rigour of Islam are part of its great power. By performing the duties of confession of faith, ritual prayer five times a day, almsgiving, fasting during the month of Ramadān, and pilgrimage to Mecca once in his lifetime, the Muslim observes the Five Pillars of Islam, and believes himself to be in God's hands and within the sphere of God's will, whatever happens. Such is the Muslim conviction of divine omnipotence that he is prepared to accept whatever comes as the will of Allāh. As the Qur'ān, the sacred book of the Muslims, says: 'No misfortune befalls except by Allāh's will.' (64.11). It is this conviction, buttressed by attempts to explain evil in terms of punishment or trial, that provides the practising Muslim with the strength to bear suffering.

A collection of prayers from the religions of the world will give some indication of the common power of devotional religion to comfort and sustain the believer in face of evil and suffering. It is a widespread belief that God or the divine powers will help the worshipper in time of need. In Hinduism we see this not only in the Avatār doctrine but in the temple cults of Vishnu or Shiva and the many lesser divinities. In Mahāyāna Buddhism we find the doctrine of grace and compassion from the Buddhas and Bodhisattvas. Judaism speaks of a covenant between God and his people, whereby they are assured of ultimate vindication. Christianity speaks of the incarnation of God's Son for the salvation of mankind, and of the grace of God available to all who turn to him. Islam speaks of Allāh, the Compassionate, the Merciful. These beliefs are certainly held to reflect real spiritual resources against evil and suffering here and now. The way in which they also involve beliefs about the ultimate destiny of man will be spelled out in the final chapter. But for the present life devotional religion can open up patterns of forgiveness, endurance and compassion, that constitute a major contribution

32

of the religions to the problem of coping with moral evil, enabling people to bear suffering, and inspiring them to relieve it.

THE WAY OF WORKS

The religions of the world have been concerned to teach the good life both by precept and example. The resources which we have so far been examining, chiefly from the point of view of the quest for liberation from the burden of existence and from moral evil, have also, in different ways and to different degrees, enabled men and women to attain to remarkable levels of sainthood. On a less exalted plane, ordinary people have experienced, through religion, the inspiration to resist temptation and live altruistically. Admittedly this has often involved the sanctions of divine punishment and reward, but the world religions have tended to develop increasingly in the direction of positive moral idealism.

In addition to the way of mystical knowledge and the way of devotion the Bhagavad Gītā speaks of the way of works. Its third chapter is traditionally known as the *karma-yoga*, the '*yoga* of action or works'. *Karma* is an important concept in Indian religion, for it is by actions with their inevitable consequences in accordance with the moral law that a man earns his place in subsequent incarnations. This theory enables men to see present suffering as the result of previous wrong. As was pointed out above (p. 22), such a context of belief suggests a response to the facts of evil at two levels—the accumulation of 'good *karma*', by which one earns a better place in the next incarnation, and the quest for release from the whole cycle of rebirth.

The two levels of response are not alternatives. Hinduism does not teach that the quest for liberation frees a man from the need to pursue right action. Whatever else a man may do to achieve salvation, he must perform his duty, as laid down in the moral order of the universe. Hence the importance in Hinduism of the notion of *dharma*, which means 'law' or 'righteousness', and refers both to the moral order and to one's duty. Thus in the Bhagavad Gītā Krishna instructs Arjuna in his duty as a member of the warrior caste. Arjuna's sense of the horror of war is partly met by the realization that it is his sacred duty to fight.

The more general account of *karma-yoga* in chapter three of the Bhagavad Gītā explains how a man must do his work in fulfilling his caste duty, just as the god does his in upholding the universe. Man's work includes the work of sacrifice to the gods, and particularly the acquisition of wisdom in order to conquer anger and desire; for it is anger and desire that make men do evil. But Krishna also teaches Arjuna to do his duty in a spirit of detachment from the fruits of action, knowing that both he and his enemies are ultimately indestructible and one with Brahman. This is the way in which the two levels of response to evil interact, making release a possibility while one is still in this life and carrying out its duties.

This emphasis on detachment, and the whole theory of release, both in this life and from the whole cycle of rebirth, might seem to militate against a lively moral sense and an active social concern. There is no denying that Hinduism has been subject to these criticisms. But there is also no denying that, especially since the nineteenth century, Hinduism has shown a considerable ability to foster selfless devotion to others. Swami Vivekānanda (1863–1902), the best known disciple of the Hindu saint Rāmakrishna (1834–86) and the founder of the Rāmakrishna Mission, claimed that the belief that every soul is one with Brahman inevitably led to love of all men and to active social care. Moreover, he insisted that practical life needed the spiritual basis which the Hindu tradition provides.

Similarly early Buddhism's quest for enlightenment is accompanied by a strong ethical sense on the part of both Buddhist monks and lay people in general. The Buddha's compassion for all caught up in the toils of suffering has already been mentioned (p. 4). Buddhism has contained from the beginning an inner drive to share with others its insight into the human dilemma and the way to overcome it. Moreover the Noble Eightfold Path itself includes the indispensable stage of 'right conduct', and high standards of personal and social morality have been taught in Buddhist lands. But one of the things that marked out the Buddha's teaching from Hinduism was his rejection of the divisive element of caste; Buddhist ethics have never been restricted by notions of caste duty such as are to be found in Krishna's advice to Arjuna in the Bhagavad Gītā.

Caste is also rejected by the Sikhs, who, as has already been pointed out (p. 31), manifested the strong ethical sense character-istic of personal monotheism. Service of one's fellow men, with-out distinction, is taught in Sikh ethics.

Later Buddhism stresses the theme of compassion in its doctrine of the Bodhisattvas, those 'Buddhas-to-be' who, on the verge of attaining Nirvāna, put off its final realization in order to help the suffering multitudes, not only by teaching them the way to enlightenment but also by relieving human suffering wherever they can.

Unlike the religions of Indian origin Confucianism, although set in the context of belief in the sanctions of heaven and the continuing influence of ancestors, was primarily concerned to teach an ethical way of life, both individual and social. Con-fucius, whose traditional dates are 551–479 B.C., taught the way of the true gentleman and the proper conduct of sons to their fathers. A later Confucian teacher, Mencius, taught the principle of humanity and justice and claimed that any man can become a saint. He expressed most clearly the Confucian view that man is by nature good. The third most important teacher of early Con-fucianism, Hsun Tzu, laid great stress on the fact that education can make men good. In the course of time, Confucianism became the state religion of China, and its classical writings and rituals attained official status in the empire. Confucianism is indeed the most obvious instance of a religion that tries to meet evil and suffering by fostering and sustaining an ordered way of life for man in society.

Returning westwards, we note that the Persian religion known as Zoroastrianism, whose dualistic views are discussed in the next chapter, taught a positive and activist ethic, encouraging men to overcome greed with contentment, envy with benevolence, strife with peace, falsehood with truth.

Judaism, with its emphasis on the holiness and righteousness of God, developed a strong moral sense. As the covenant partner of a holy God Israel believed herself called to obey the Torah, the law of God, which covered every aspect of life. The Ten

Commandments prescribe the outline of the law, but the early books of the Hebrew Bible are remarkable for their detailed concern for the stranger, the poor and the weak. Moreover, the great prophets of Israel, such as Hosea and Jeremiah, understood the will of God and obedience to God first and foremost in ethical terms: 'I desire mercy and not sacrifice' (Hos. 6.6). Modern Judaism is equally notable in the quality of ethical life, especially family life, which it fosters.

It is often claimed that Jesus sharpened the demands of the Jewish law, while at the same time continuing the emphasis of the Hebrew prophets on inner dispositions as much as outward acts. The example of Jesus and the revelation of the nature of God which it was understood to express, led to a characteristic emphasis, in Christianity, on self-giving love. This quality has been manifested throughout Christian history in such figures as St Francis or, in our own time, Mother Teresa of Calcutta. It is a feature of Christianity that ethical action, whether that of the saints or that of ordinary Christians, has been regarded not as a condition of salvation nor as a means to it, but rather as the natural expression of faith in response to human need. Modern Christianity has included a marked emphasis on social action, as in the Christian Socialist movement and in the political theology currently embraced by the World Council of Churches.

Islam resembles Judaism in placing great emphasis on the revealed law of God. It prescribes a comprehensive moral system for the conduct of individual and social life. This is known as the *shariah*, the pathway to be trodden in order to please God. Aspects of its code, such as those relating to the position of women have been criticized, but, as is the case with other living religions, Islam has experienced the force of self-criticism and reform. An example of this is the social idealism of Muhammad Iqbāl (1873–1938), one of the leaders of the Muslim League in India. He regarded it as a distinctive aim of Islam to 'demolish all the artificial and pernicious distinctions of caste, creed, colour and economic status'.

Whatever one's view of evil and suffering, there are many human ills that can, in practical terms, be averted, mitigated or relieved by ethical teaching and action. Some forms of religion are, admittedly, themselves open to ethical criticism. But a comprehensive survey of world religion will reveal many morally creative ways of combating evil and suffering. At the very least one can say that the religions have inspired much human goodness and compassionate ethical action. Certainly the religions have no monopoly in this area of ethical response, as we saw when looking at Camus and at the Marxists. But the ways of life encouraged and made possible by religion, it could be claimed, are often enhanced by the specifically religious contexts of devotion and of ultimate meaning and hope in which the world faiths place them.

It is very difficult to compare the ethical ideals of the different religions. But a much needed enterprise in Religious Studies would be a careful comparison, say, of the value of compassion in Buddhism with that of love (*agapé*) in Christianity. One element in such a comparison would be a study of the development of the notion of sacrifice.

THE WAY OF SACRIFICE

Sacrifice is one of the most common forms of religious ritual act. Indeed the history of the theistic religions is in large part a history of the refinement and spiritualization of sacrificial ideas. In early religion in non-literate tribal societies, in the classical world of Greece and Rome and at the cultural beginnings of the world religions, we find propitiatory sacrifices, allegedly appeasing the wrath of the gods, sometimes even taking the form of human sacrifice. At the same time we find many examples of simple offerings to God or to the gods, for example the first-fruits of the harvest, in order to preserve their favour and continuing help. Then there are expiatory sacrifices, by which men try to atone for their sins, to make, as it were, some ritual act of reparation. There are also communion sacrifices, in which the worshippers share a sacramental meal, thereby identifying themselves with, say, the dying and rising god of the mystery cults. Lastly, we find more ethical ideas of self-sacrifice emerging in the world religions.

One of the most striking examples of the recognition of the

value of self-sacrifice is to be found in Mahāyāna Buddhism. With its non-theistic roots Buddhism has no place for sacrifice to the gods, but in the developments of the Bodhisattva doctrine we find not only examples of self-sacrifice, as in the story of the Bodhisattva who gave himself to a tigress as food for her starving young, but also the theory that in putting off his own final attainment of Nirvāna for the sake of others a Bodhisattva is to identify himself with the suffering of men and to take it upon himself:

A Bodhisattva resolves: I take upon myself the burden of all suffering ... I have made the vow to save all beings ... The whole world of living beings I must rescue from the terrors of birth, of old age, of sickness, of death and rebirth, of all kinds of moral offence, of all states of woe, of the whole cycle of birth-and-death, of the jungle of false views ...[5]

The idea of the value of suffering borne on others' behalf appears in Judaism at the time of the exile in the sixth century B.C. The prophet known as Deutero-Isaiah, who was responsible for chapters 40–55 of the book of Isaiah in the Hebrew Bible, envisaged a figure known as the Suffering Servant, who 'has borne our griefs and carried our sorrows ... But he was wounded for our transgressions, he was bruised for our iniquities; upon him was the chastisement that made us whole, and with his stripes we are healed' (Isa., 53.4–5). This idea, that an individual, perhaps symbolic of the remnant of Israel, can atone for the sins of the people by taking suffering upon himself, was one of the ethically creative ways in which traditional ideas of sacrifice came to be spiritualized and moralized. A further development took place in the period of the Maccabees (second century B.C.), who led a revolt against the Syrian rulers. The large number of Jewish martyrs of that time came to be regarded as having given their lives to atone for the people's sins.

These ideas were taken up in Christianity, which identified Christ with the Suffering Servant, and saw in his death on the Cross the ultimate atoning sacrifice. As such, it was held to

[5] J. W. Bowker, *Problems of Suffering in Religions of the World*, (C.U.P.), pp. 264–5.

have abolished the need for any further sacrifices, and so in the Christian liturgies sacrifice became a purely spiritual thing, a self-dedication of the worshippers to God, and a spiritual communion with Christ by which the effects of his perfect sacrifice were held to be made available to Christians. These ideas were not found easy to grasp and several conflicting doctrines of atonement were developed in the Christian Church; but the special force in Christian experience has always stemmed from the belief that it was God incarnate who had entered into human suffering, taking it upon himself and demonstrating his costly reconciling love. The idea that in this way God takes upon himself responsibility for the evil in the world, while not explaining the presence of that evil, has been felt to have great moral and spiritual force in enabling Christians to cope with evil themselves.

The notion of redemptive suffering is not central to Islam, but we do find it appearing in the context of Shī'ite martyrdom. The division between Sunni and Shī'a Islam goes back to the question of the correct successors to Muhammad. The Shī'ites look back to their martyrs, Alī, Hasan and Husain, as being by their sufferings in a special position to intercede for sinners. But the idea of a suffering God is alien to the Muslim tradition with its emphasis on the omnipotence and sovereignty of Allāh, although it is interesting to learn that modern Shī'ites in dialogue with Christians have remarked that in this respect they have not finished with the problem of suffering.[6]

In summary, it is worth stressing that self-sacrifice and self-sacrificing love are not the only lasting values to be found in the development of ideas of sacrifice in the history of religions. They may represent the highest point of the religions' practical response to suffering. But the notion of expiation, the felt need to make some act of atonement and of reparation for genuine guilt, is also an aspect of the life of persons enhanced by those religions which set men in the context of a relation to a personal God. To that extent, it could be argued, the problem of moral evil as well as that of suffering is met most profoundly in and through the notion of sacrifice.

[6] J. Moltmann, *The Crucified God*, (S.C.M. Press), p. 158.

39

3

EXPLAINING EVIL AND SUFFERING

However varied and however profound the ways of coping with evil and suffering recommended and exemplified in the religions of the world, many religious minds are still left with the nagging 'why' questions. Why are things like this? Why is there so much innocent suffering? Why are men so wicked? Why are they permitted to cause such suffering to others?

We now survey the different answers which have been suggested by the religions to questions such as these. It has already been pointed out that not all religions give rise to these questions, but that they are felt particularly acutely in the theistic religions, where belief in God is central. It is also true that within the theistic religions such questioning has sometimes been discouraged as rebellious or even blasphemous. Nevertheless the urge to try to understand has nearly always prevailed, the doubts and questions sooner or later coming to the surface and demanding an answer. The bare appeal to faith and trust has not been felt to be enough. In every theistic religion we find some explanatory framework in terms of which the presence and extent of evil and suffering can be understood.

EXPLANATION IN NON-THEISTIC RELIGIONS

Before looking at the various explanations offered in the theistic religions, let us recall how differently the facts of suffering present themselves in the non-theistic religions. We have already had occasion to compare the attitude of early Buddhism to the world's suffering with that of certain non-religious world views. But whereas it is the problem of evil which often makes men reject theistic religion, no such line of argument appears in Buddhist thought. The Buddha had nothing to say about the gods; he simply faced the facts of suffering, offered a diagnosis of their root cause, and recommended a way of release. This lack of interest in the 'why' questions remains characteristic of later Buddhism. We have noted the profound ways in which Mahāyāna Buddhism sought to cope with suffering through serene faith, compassion and self-sacrifice but the Bodhisattva doctrine still raised no ultimate questions concerning the meaning or purpose of the world's suffering.

The same holds true of Taoism. There is less sense of the radical and all-pervasive nature of suffering in this passive Chinese mystical religion. The eternal principle is there underlying nature. Men have only to yield themselves to its harmony in order to find peace. The diagnosis may be more optimistic and the cure less arduous than that of Buddhism, but in neither case do we find the demand for explanation.

MAGICAL AND PRIMITIVE VIEWS

In the beginnings of theistic religions it is hard to separate religion from magic. All primitive beliefs have a curious rationality in that, within the system, say, of magical belief, everything that happens is quite intelligible. Anything that goes wrong can be attributed to the malevolence of some agent exercising hidden powers; it might be another human being, or perhaps the dead, or perhaps some spiritual power that has been offended. As we move from a world of belief where such powers are thought to be amenable to spells and counter-magic to a world of belief where prayers and sacrifices to appease the gods are thought to be more appropriate, we begin to move from the world of magic to that of religion; for the powers responsible for human ills are no longer thought to be subject to human control. But in either case the evil experienced is well understood, since ill-will, revenge and punishment are intelligible notions to human beings.

Even where a tribal religion acknowledges the supreme God as basically good, evil and suffering can still be attributed to the activity of lesser deities. Thus the Yoruba in Nigeria have 1,700 divinities connected with different natural phenomena and human experiences, good and bad.

It is quite understandable how a member of such a tribe, when confronted with scientific explanations of natural phenomena, feels a great loss of intelligibility in his world. To confine explanation of the collapse of his hut and the death of his family to pointing out the eating away of the joists by termites is to render the whole episode meaningless. He wants to know who sent the termites.

In cultures where explanations in terms of intentional action begin to lose their grip one sometimes finds a transfer of religious sentiment to impersonal forces: we mentioned the fact that in the Greek and Roman world it was sometimes believed that the gods themselves were subject to fate (p. 20). Fate (or fortune) itself then became an ultimate explanation and the focus of a cult. Such reactions could easily take a non-religious form, as in Lucretius' philosophy. A corollary of this kind of view is, of course, that it is a mistake to look for an explanation of evil and suffering, except in terms of the regular working of natural laws; for according to such views there *is* no other explanation.

DUALISTIC VIEWS

The history of religions, however, is the history of mankind's continuing attempts to find ultimate meaning behind the ambiguous phenomena of nature and human experience. One solution to the problem of evil and suffering is to see two equally ultimate principles behind both good and evil. This view is known as dualism.

The chief example of an ultimate dualism in religion is that of Zoroastrianism in Iran, or Persia, as it used to be called. Its representatives today include the Parsis in India, particularly the large Parsi community in Bombay. The dates of Zoroaster (or Zarathustra) are much disputed, the traditional dates being 628–551 B.C. Some of his hymns (the Gathas) are incorporated in the Zoroastrian scriptures, the Avesta. While the creation and all good come from Ahura Mazda, the 'wise Lord', there is an uncreated spiritual force working against him. This is the source of all evil. The world, although itself a good creation, has

42

become the battleground of good and evil. Although the forces of good and evil are both eternal in the sense of being un-created and without a beginning, Zoroastrian belief is not pessi-mistic about the outcome of this struggle. The good will finally overcome and destroy the evil.

Dualistic elements are also to be found in some strands of devotional Hinduism, particularly in Shaivite belief, that is, among the followers of the god Shiva. Shiva is both creator and destroyer, showing now a benevolent, now a terrifying aspect. He is often accompanied by his consort Kālī, who represents the darker side of the divine power. Animal sacrifice to propitiate the goddess is still offered in the temple of Kālī in Calcutta. Shiva is a paradoxical figure, reflecting the ambiguities of creation and destruction in human life and experience. His creative power is to be seen in the stone phallus (the lingam) found in all Shaivite temples, and in the exuberant dance by which he is held to have created the world. Strangely Shiva also inspires asceticism, in imitation of the *yoga*, by which he main-tains the world in being. Clearly the Shiva cult represents a very different solution to the problem of evil from that of Zoro-astrianism. To see present ambiguities as reflecting the struggle between two ultimate principles, good and evil, is one thing; to see them both as included within the one divine source of all life quite another. It is not surprising that Zoroastrianism sees God in highly ethical terms, while there is a tendency in some forms of Hinduism to see God as beyond good and evil. Never-theless, from the point of view of the need to explain evil and suffering these two religions have in common the sense that the good and evil which men experience derive from the ultimate nature of things.

A third, and again very different, form of dualism is to be found in the religion of Mani, a Persian, whose traditional dates are A.D. 216–77. It is claimed that Zoroastrian, Christian and Buddhist influences lie behind the emergence of Manichaeism, in which it was taught that matter is an eternal principle and the source of all evil in the world, and that true religion consists in the purification and release of the soul from its entanglement in matter. Once again the presence of evil and suffering is traced back to an ultimate principle, but it is clear that Manichaeism, in treating matter as an eternal evil substance, is rejecting the fundamental doctrine of the creation of the world, which Zoroastrianism shares with Christianity.

Judaism, Christianity and Islam (and, in India, the Vaishnavite form of devotional Hinduism) have consistently rejected all dualistic solutions to the problem of evil, at the cost of retaining that problem right in their heart. The reasons why the developed theistic religions tend to reject an ultimate dualism are both religious and philosophical. Religiously speaking, the inner drive towards an ethical monotheism makes it more and more difficult to affirm equally ultimate powers independent of God, thus compromising his omnipotence. Philosophically speaking, the inner drive towards the recognition of an infinite source of all there is militates against any ultimate dualism. The combination of these religious and philosophical pressures has led the theistic religions, both in their scriptures and in their theologies, to affirm doctrines of creation, in which all finite beings depend wholly on the creative will of God. Similar pressures can be seen at work in other strands of Hinduism, especially the philosophical schools which base their teaching on the Upanishads. Non-dualist Vedānta may not have developed a doctrine of creation, but its uncompromising monism shows a comparable tendency towards recognition of a single ultimate and absolute reality.

In the context of the development of Christian doctrine it was the Platonic philosophy which enabled the Church Fathers, and especially Augustine of Hippo (A.D. 354–430) to reject dualism and affirm the goodness of all creation. On this view evil is not a substance in its own right, but rather a corruption or perversion of what is inherently good, or else it results from a clash between elements each in itself good. This view does not solve the problem of evil; it simply rules out dualism.

The ease, however, with which the religious mind can take refuge in dualism is to be seen in the re-emergence of dualistic belief from time to time in the history of Christianity, as in the case of the Albigenses in southern France in the late twelfth and early thirteenth centuries A.D. The ferocity with which they

44

were suppressed in the Albigensian Crusade shows how the orthodox Christian Church could be touched on the raw by the recrudescence of dualism.

THE DEVIL AND THE FALL OF MAN

It might be thought that belief in the devil suggests, after all, a dualistic solution to the problem of explaining evil even in the monotheistic faiths; for in most monotheistic religions evil spirits are held to exist, and to be responsible both for moral temptation and for physical suffering, sometimes even for death. But, unlike the dualistic systems, the monotheistic religions invariably treat the devil as a creature, a fallen angel or spirit, who has himself revolted against God. Consequently an ultimate dualism is firmly denied. The devil, too, is a corrupted being, originally good. The cost of such denial, however, is that many of the 'why' questions which arise in connection with human wrong-doing arise also in respect of the devil. Why did he turn away from God? Why is he permitted to wreak such havoc in the world and in the lives of men? Indeed the problem is made much worse if the devil is regarded as incapable of redemption. Such a view, despite the intentions of monotheism, seems to introduce a dualistic element, a permanent surd, into creation after all.

The development of the idea of Satan in Judaism is very complex. He appears mainly in the later books of the Hebrew Bible, as in the prologue to the book of Job, where he seems a respectable figure in the court of God charged with the task of testing God's servants. Much later he was identified with the serpent in the Garden of Eden story who tempted Eve to eat the forbidden fruit. Later Jewish demonology was taken up in the New Testament in the story of Jesus' temptations, and the powers of Satan were seen at work in the demoniacs cured by Jesus. In the theology of John there is a kingdom of darkness, in principle overcome by (but still warring against) the kingdom of light. Paul pictures the present world as under the power of astrological forces: thrones and dominations, principalities and powers. Many New Testament writings envisage a last battle,

45

like the one in Zoroastrian belief, where the devil and his angels are finally cast down.

In the development of Christian theology one dominant strand, associated with the name of Augustine, taught that the state of the world, from which Christ came to rescue men, was caused by the fall of man in the Garden of Eden through temptation by the devil. The result of this first sin was expulsion from the garden, the necessity of pain and toil, and the fact of death. The state of original sin was thenceforth the common state of man, and the world was permitted to fall under Satan's influence. Satan's power was broken through the sacrificial death of Christ on the Cross; from then on men were to be drawn into the sphere of redemption by being united with Christ by the Spirit, and either in time or in eternity this new kingdom of God would be universally established, and once again God would be all in all. This picture dominated the Christian mind for many centuries, and had powerful explanatory force in enabling men to understand the present facts of evil and suffering.

A fallen angel also appears in the theology of Islam, drawing, no doubt, on the Judaeo-Christian ideas. The Qur'ān speaks of the angel Iblis, who resented the place of Adam in creation. He and his minions were permitted by God to remain in being as tempters to test men on earth, but such is Muslim faith in the omnipotence and sovereignty of Allāh that Iblis never attained the significance in Islam that Satan came to have in Augustinian Christianity.

Such developments within the context of these monotheistic faiths have much in common with demonology throughout the history of religions. Evil spirits abound in tribal religion, and often the fact of evil is attributed to a particular personal source. Thus the Vugusu in Kenya 'say that there is an evil divinity which God created good, but later on turned against Him and began to do evil'.[1] Hinduism has many demons. Shiva is represented as Lord over the demons. Vaishnavites, by contrast, delight in stories of Rāma or Krishna entering into battle with the demons and defeating them. Early Buddhism tells of

---

[1] John Mbiti, *African Religions and Philosophy* (Heinemann), p. 204.

the Buddha's spiritual conflict with Māra, the tempter, in the course of his quest for enlightenment.

It is very easy for the Indian religions, especially in their more philosophical and mystical forms, to regard these stories as mythology, expressing in symbolic and figurative form the realities of temptation, evil and suffering in human life. Of course, to treat them self-consciously as mythology is to deprive them of any explanatory power. Only if taken literally can demons constitute an explanation of evil. But we have already seen how Buddhism is not particularly interested in explaining evil in that sense and in Hinduism there are strong tendencies, either to press the source of destructive power right back into the supreme deity, or else to regard both good and evil as aspects of the illusory world, transcended in the higher mystical states.

Christian theology today is divided on the question whether or not to treat the demonology of its scriptures and tradition as mythology and as a culture-bound figurative expression of the reality and seriousness of the evil that afflicts human beings in the world. The view that the devil and evil spirits are mythological figures is supported by the recognition of the facts of cultural change and the conviction that no religion need be fixated in the frameworks of belief of thousands of years ago. On any view many of the phenomena once attributed to demon possession are now explicable in terms of modern medical science. Nor need the arguments against literal belief in the devil affect fundamental beliefs like belief in God; for no reflective monotheist could regard the case for an infinite creative source of all being and value as symmetrical with the case for a personal devil.

It has to be admitted that the presence of evil can be experienced in such a way as strongly to suggest the influence of malevolent agencies. It is not surprising that the history of religions contains so much demonological belief. But psychological knowledge and a conviction of the incoherence of belief in the devil in a total monotheistic world view combine to make many Christians resist the easy resort to belief in evil spirits. Such belief, it may be added, can lead to fears, fantasies and obsessions, which greatly increase the sum of human ills, as

47

writers like Lucretius have often pointed out.

It is recognized by modern Christians who accept this line of argument that, once the devil is regarded only as a symbolic figure, then the Augustinian framework of explanation for the presence of evil in the world collapses. The doctrines of the fall of man and of original sin become symbolic of man's condition. There is no longer any explanatory force in talk of the devil.

SUFFERING AS DIVINE PUNISHMENT, TESTING AND DISCIPLINE

Perhaps the simplest religious answer to the 'why' questions which trouble theists is that suffering constitutes divine punishment. This can be regarded as one among several possible explanations of suffering. In tribal religion, for instance, suffering might also be simply the result of a neighbour's malice. But in the history of monotheism explanations in terms of divine punishment tend to take on universal scope, lesser agencies being regarded as instruments of the divine purpose. On this view suffering is always deserved, and indeed evidence of guilt, since had there been no guilt God would not have punished. In early stages of religious development this framework of explanation was applied corporately rather than individually: the nation suffered because of its idolatry; the sins of the fathers were visited upon the children.

Clear examples of this view are to be found in the Hebrew Bible. It is the view of the Deuteronomic historian, who tells the story of the kings of Israel and Judah, and of the fate of the people at the hands of foreign invaders, precisely in terms of divine reward and punishment. As a more individualist attitude comes to prevail in the later books of the Hebrew Bible, we find a similar inference from suffering to guilt being made in the case of Job by his so-called comforters. They assume that his troubles are evidence of guilt.

The Qur'ān also teaches that suffering can be punishment for sin, but, appearing so much later in the history of religions, it does not attempt to meet the problem of innocent suffering by denying its existence. For Judaism and Christianity had long since had to reckon with the fact of innocent suffering. The book

48

of Job makes it clear that the orthodoxy of his comforters was false comfort; and the lasting power of the book of Job consists in the poignancy with which it brings out the seriousness of the problem of innocent suffering. We have already seen how Judaism developed the idea that, far from being evidence of guilt, suffering could acquire redemptive significance. This has been, of course, a central notion in Christianity with its focus on the Cross of Christ, but it is interesting to note that Jesus had explicitly to reject the older view that suffering was punishment for sin. He instructed his disciples not to think that the people on whom the tower of Siloam fell must have been particularly wicked (Luke 13.4). Nevertheless, both in Judaism and in Christianity the belief in suffering as punishment and as evidence of guilt has had a strong tendency to recur, especially at the level of popular belief.

Where the idea of suffering as punishment was felt to be inadequate, another explanation could replace or supplement it, namely, the idea of suffering as a divine test or trial of faith. We have already come across this idea in the case of Job; for it is God who permits Satan to test his servant Job. The idea that the good man is somehow purged or refined in the fire of suffering is quite common in the history of religions. Persecution could be regarded in this light. This was true of the Jewish martyrs under Syrian rule and of the early Christian martyrs, like Polycarp, in the second century A.D., although in the Christian case ideas of sharing in Christ's suffering and bearing witness to the faith played a more central role.

It is in Islam that the idea of suffering as a test of faith acquires particular importance. The Qur'ān makes this explicit: 'We shall test your steadfastness with fear and famine, with loss of life and property and crops. Give good news to those who endure with fortitude, who in adversity say: "We belong to Allāh, and to Him we shall return." On such men will be Allāh's blessing and mercy.' (ii.150ff.). Muslims, then, should expect to be subject to the trial of suffering. It is not surprising to find this emphasis in Islam with its conviction of the omnipotence and inscrutable will of God. For the Muslim some such explanation *must* be true. But for many Christians the idea that

49

suffering, especially its extreme form, is intended by God as a test of faith casts grave doubts on the goodness of God.

Related to the idea of suffering as a trial of faith is the idea that suffering can be explained as a necessary part of the process of discipline by which character is formed and developed. The book of Proverbs in the Hebrew Bible says: 'The Lord disciplines those whom he loves' (3.12). This verse is quoted in the New Testament by the author of the letter to the Hebrews, who continues: 'It is for discipline that you have to endure. God is treating you as sons; for what son is there whom his father does not discipline?' (12.7). Similar arguments are also to be found in the Qur'ān as well as the bare appeal to the idea of trial or test. Such a line of argument can have a great deal of force in relation to many of the tribulations of life, but hardly to the extremities of human suffering. Once again, in relation to such major disasters as earthquakes and floods or to human wickedness on the scale of Auschwitz, it seems quite immoral to speak either of trial or discipline.

Nevertheless, reference to the function of pain and suffering in the development of character and personality and in the fostering of virtues such as fortitude and compassion is a common feature of modern attempts at theodicy (justifying the ways of God to man) by philosophical theologians. Thus we find Professor John Hick, in his book *Evil and the God of Love*, (Fontana) arguing that it makes sense to see the world with all its potentialities for harm as well as good as 'a vale of soul-making', a context in which personal creatures can be fashioned and schooled in the virtues. Without suffering there would be no scope for the exercise of character and perseverance, or even enduring, self-sacrificial love. Few of the values of interpersonal life would ever emerge and grow in a world in which there was no suffering.

It seems likely that such considerations would make the presence of some suffering in the world intelligible and justifiable. But quite apart from the inability of this view to account for the extremities of human suffering, it presents us in any case, so critics have argued, with an over-moralistic picture of the world. Granted that compassion is an excellent virtue in response to human suffering, it is difficult to see that particular cases of suffering, or even the general structures of the world which make suffering an ever-present possibility, could be justifiably brought about in order to give scope for compassion. This type of theodicy still places the Creator in a morally questionable light. Another objection is that to see the world as a vale of soul-making is in any case too narrow a world view. It fails to do justice to the profusion, variety and exuberant energy of the physical, animal and human creation.

It is interesting to contrast these views of suffering as punishment, test or discipline with the pervasive notion in Indian religion of the automatic consequences of human action. The concept of *karma-saṃsāra* gives intelligibility to any present experience since it is regarded as the consequence of action, if not in this, then in previous lives. One's position and fortune in this life are the result of one's actions in earlier incarnations, and one's purpose in observing the law of righteousness (*dharma*) now is to accumulate 'good *karma*' and to achieve a better incarnation next time. Of course the Indian religions were not content with this level of response. We have seen how they aim to set men free from the whole round of birth and rebirth. But the doctrine of *karma* has a certain explanatory force in the face of puzzlement about the present distribution of suffering. There is an impersonal law of moral cause and effect written into the nature of things.

HUMAN FREEDOM

By far the most common explanation, within the theistic religions, of a great deal of evil and suffering is based on the fact of human freedom. If at least one of God's purposes in creation was to establish a world of personal beings over against himself and able to enter into personal relations with each other and with him, then they must have been created free to choose either good or evil. The only alternative was a world of puppets, programmed to act rightly, and that would not have been a world of persons. Indeed the notion of acting rightly would have no application, since moral goodness necessarily involves free

51

choice. The possibility of wrong choice, therefore, had to be allowed. Moral evil and the suffering it causes are to be explained as resulting from this necessary condition of a world of persons. Examples of this argument in a number of religions and discussion of its rationality will be found in the next chapter. Suffice it to say here, first, that even if it works it accounts for only some of the world's ills, namely, those which depend on the exercise of free will; and secondly, given the enormous amount and terrible nature of human wickedness and its consequences, we have still to ask Ivan Karamazov's question whether creation at such a cost is worth it.

THE NATURE AND FUNCTION OF THE PHYSICAL WORLD

The physical and mental suffering brought about by natural causes such as earthquakes, floods, droughts and plagues cannot be explained by reference to human free will. There are also innumerable accidents which cause grievous hurt and loss to human beings. Again it is the structure of the natural world that makes the results of human wickedness so terrible for innocent victims. Our century knows only too well how the high threshold of pain in human beings makes it possible to invent and carry out horrific tortures.

These facts are often not faced squarely at early stages in the history of religions. Where the natural world is seen as a mask covering the intentional activities of hidden spiritual powers, the quest for explanation is pushed back from the apparent structures of things to the agencies believed to lie behind them. In more sophisticated and developed theological systems the more hostile elements of nature are sometimes believed to be the result, not of the physical world's God-given structure, but of the devil's interference. Only because the whole world has fallen under the devil's dominion do pain and suffering take the form they do.

Two converging factors make this a very difficult position to hold. From the side of theology comes further reflection on the doctrine of creation, and the implausibility of taking literally the idea of a devil who is on the one hand beyond the possibility of redemption and on the other permitted to interfere with the creation to the extent of corrupting its very physical properties. From the side of scientific knowledge comes reflection on the properties and powers of the substances and fundamental energies disclosed to modern physics and chemistry, and the implausibility of thinking these to be corrupted or distorted rather than original.

The philosophical theologian, therefore, working within the context of belief in an infinite Creator spirit, is bound to address his thoughts to the physical world as it is increasingly known to modern science, taking its structures and energies and all their properties and powers as God-given. The main question regarding pain and suffering is then recognized to be: why does God create a physical world which, for all its wonders and beauties, can also cause untold harm to sentient beings?

The answer which is to be illustrated and examined in chapter five is that the properties of nature which cause harm to creatures are precisely the same fundamental properties which make possible an organic world of growth and change, the context of personal being and development. In a nutshell, you cannot have one without the other. If this argument can be made out, then we have an explanation, albeit somewhat austere, of the facts of innocent suffering. Of course Ivan Karamazov's question remains here again unanswered.

CREATION IN PROCESS

The explanations sketched briefly in the last two sections could be given in the context of any monotheistic religion, where it has become necessary to relate the findings of modern science to the belief that the natural world possesses God-given structures. But both 'the free will defence', as it is commonly called, and the explanation of suffering as a by-product of structures and energies necessary to the production of life and growth, are, in a sense, backward-looking explanations. They attempt to show, that is, why the creation must contain possibilities of wrong choice and physical suffering in the first place. But there is another line of argument, based on the idea that

53

creation is an on-going process leading to a future goal, which also needs to be taken into account. This line of argument, which will be illustrated and explored in our final chapter, cannot explain why evil and suffering exist in present experience. Only arguments pointing to the necessary conditions of the original creation carry explanatory force. But reflection on the ultimate future goal of creation can perhaps help with the problem of justification—the problem, that is, of showing why the great cost of creation in present evil and suffering is worthwhile.

Two preliminary points about this emphasis on the future goal of creation can be made here. In the first place only those religions which have come to see the universe as a single developing process towards an ultimate future goal can deploy this kind of argument. Religions which regard the cosmos as an ever-recurring cycle of growth and decay cannot place any great stress on the future in their quest for justification.

In the second place, it has to be recognized that even a religion like Christianity with its stress on the centrality and meaningfulness of history, has not been able to make the most of its insight into creation as a continuing process so long as it has held to the Augustinian picture of a perfect creation in the past, from which mankind and the world have fallen away. Only when this picture is abandoned, and the creative process seen rather as the gradual fashioning of a world of persons, whose perfection will be realized only in an ultimate future, can the kind of theodicy which we are about to explore in detail acquire its full force.

4

MORAL EVIL AND HUMAN FREEDOM

Our task in this chapter is to examine the place of free will in the religions of the world, especially in the theistic religions, since they alone are able to regard free will as a gift, and thus to point to the reason for this gift as an explanation for the possibility of moral evil in the world. The harmful use of man's freedom is, admittedly, not universally regarded as a morally reprehensible thing; some religions see it more as a matter of ignorance than sin. But on any view the consequences of human action can be devastating, and much of the world's suffering is caused by what human beings freely do.

FREE WILL IN INDIAN RELIGION

It will readily be apparent why little is said about Buddhism in this chapter. The Buddha certainly taught that men are free and able to do something about the situation in which they find themselves, but he thought that the prevalence of harmful action was due to ignorance. Men generally did not realize that they were acting on the basis of a universal craving which inevitably brought suffering in its train. When this was pointed out to them, they could begin to take the necessary steps to free themselves from its pervasive power. But the main reason why Buddhism cannot help us in our present inquiry is that, as a non-theistic religion, it cannot regard men's freedom as a gift, intended for a purpose.

But Indian religion, even in its more theistic forms, makes very little use of the idea of freedom as a gift. There were some interesting disputes among the disciples of Rāmānuja, the eleventh century Hindu theologian, about the place of free action in man's appropriation of God's grace—the 'monkey' school

55

holding that men have actively to cling to God like baby monkeys clinging to their mothers, the 'cat' school holding that God takes hold of a man as a cat takes hold of her kittens by the scruff of the neck. In general, however, without denying the reality of God, Hinduism has tended to regard the consequences of human action as falling under the impersonal automatic operation of the law of *karma*. The question why the world has such a structure has not been pressed. This is a reflection of the difference between eastern and western doctrines of creation. The east has lacked the west's persistent feeling that there must be a morally satisfying reason for the way things are with the world and with man.

ZOROASTRIANISM

Man's freedom and ability to choose between good and evil is a basic doctrine of Zoroastrianism. But in the context of an ultimate dualism, the problem is very different from that of explaining why evil exists at all. For Zoroastrianism that is already explained: there exists from all eternity an ultimate evil spirit. The only thing that the reality of human freedom is called upon to explain is why men sometimes choose the evil and submit to the promptings of the evil one.

JUDAISM

Judaism, too, with its strong ethical sense, manifested in the law of Moses and in the Covenant between God and his people, was very conscious of man's freedom to obey or to rebel. Its teachings about divine punishment and divine forgiveness presuppose this. The need to turn back to God, and hence the ability to turn back to him, are stressed by the prophets and the wisdom writers of ancient Israel. But it is surprising how little use was made of the free will argument in justifying the ways of God to man either by the writers of the Hebrew Bible or by the rabbis, or indeed in modern Judaism. It is in fact alien to the spirit of Judaism to try to justify the ways of God to man except in terms of punishment, trial, or the opportunity for vicarious suffering. The medieval Jewish philosopher, Maimonides, in his *Guide of the Perplexed*, did spell out the causes of evil in the world, attributing the larger part of it to human action, but he did not examine the role of human freedom in the creation or stress its necessity if God's plan in creation was to be realized at all.

CHRISTIANITY

Christianity shares the basic Jewish conviction that man is created free to live in harmony with his Creator or to turn against him. But in the course of its development, both in the early centuries and in modern times, Christianity has become more conscious both of the problems and of the possibilities of emphasizing human freedom.

To take the problems first: we have already shown how, for Augustinian Christianity, much of the weight of explanation for the facts of evil is carried by the doctrine of the fall of man. Now free will certainly plays an important role in this account. Adam acted freely in succumbing to temptation, just as Satan had previously acted freely in turning against God. In general, Augustine is quite clear that wickedness is 'perversion of the will when it turns aside from you, O God ... and veers towards things of the lowest order ...' (*Confessions*, Bk VII. 16). But another set of considerations prevents Augustine from giving too much significance to the free will argument in theodicy. These are the considerations pointing in the direction of a predestinarian view. Belief in the sovereignty of God over his creation, and especially belief in the priority and sufficiency of God's action in redemption, have led many Christian thinkers, including Augustine and Calvin, to minimize or to deny the reality of human freedom, once the fall had occurred. Free choice can still play a part in explaining the possibility of a fall in the first place, but, once fallen, mankind is helpless until God acts out of pure grace to restore the situation. Fierce controversy took place between Augustine and Pelagius for example, and between Luther and Erasmus at the time of the Reformation, about the scope of human freedom left under the conditions of the fall; but it has undoubtedly been widely held that fallen man can

57

do nothing to restore his broken relation with God (implicitly siding, therefore, with the 'cat' school rather than the 'monkey' school among the disciples of Rāmānuja).

There is still room for disagreement about the reality and significance of human freedom in man's dealings with his fellows. Theologians have always wanted to retain enough freedom to justify the ascription of moral responsibility to people, but within the Augustinian framework it has been difficult to place a great deal of emphasis on the importance of freedom in the development of human personality over against God.

Where the Augustinian framework has been decisively rejected, however, the way becomes clear for a much greater deployment of the free will argument in theodicy. Professor John Hick has shown how this non-Augustinian strand in Christian theology can be traced back to Irenaeus, the second century Bishop of Lyons. Irenaeus rejected the idea that man was created perfect in the beginning, and taught, instead, that in the infancy of the human race it was not possible for man to receive the perfection which God intends for him. Rather, by training and growth in the knowledge of good and evil man reached the stage when he was capable of receiving the knowledge of God in Christ; and the process of education will continue until the final consummation. Man's freedom and the possibility of wrong choice are now seen as necessary features of the creative process, on the analogy of their place in a child's growth to maturity through experience and correction. Within the Irenaean framework it can still be argued that man's actual state of alienation is such that he cannot escape from the structures of self-destruction without God's help, but this conviction need not detract from the recognition of the necessary role of freedom in the creation of persons.

The tension between Augustinian and Irenaean strands in the Christian tradition is nowhere more clearly seen than in the thought of Thomas Aquinas, the great medieval systematizer of Christian theology. Aquinas' basic solution to the problem of evil is that God 'permits certain defects in particular effects, that the perfect good of the universe may not be hindered; for if all evil were prevented, much good would be absent from the universe' (*Summa Theologiae*, 1a. 22.2). Applied to the case of free will, this principle means that God permits the misuse of freedom, since if it were prevented there would be no free personal creatures to learn to love and respond to their Creator. But the notion of divine permission is a very difficult one to incorporate within an overall picture of divine sovereignty and providence, and we find Aquinas struggling at this point, trying like many other Christians to have it both ways: 'whatsoever divine providence ordains to happen infallibly and of necessity happens infallibly and of necessity; and what the divine providence plans to happen contingently happens contingently'. But it is difficult to see how the 'planning' of contingent happenings makes sense.

At least it can be seen from the different views that have been sketched that Christianity has the resources for developing a theodicy based on the necessary role of free will in the creation and growth of personal relations with each other and with God. Freed from the encumbrances of belief in an original state of perfection, from which men fell away, such a theodicy can draw on the full explanatory force of the necessary permission of freedom and its consequences if the creative purpose is to be realized. This element in theodicy will be all the more important where literal belief in the devil is renounced together with what limited explanatory force the devil had.

ISLAM

The tension between divine omnipotence and human freedom is also to be found in the history of Muslim belief. Just because Islam has always been more conscious of the sovereignty and omnipotence of God than of anything else, it has tended to foster determinist and predestinarian views even more uncompromisingly than Christianity. This is certainly the impression given by the tradition of Muhammad's life and teaching. But we have also seen that the Qur'ān speaks of suffering as divine punishment, and this implies that God had given men freedom to obey or disobey. Sufi mystics were very insistent on this: '... our sense of guilt is evidence of free will'. So in Muslim

59

theology resort was made to the concept of divine permission, as it was in Christian theology. Thus in the ninth century A.D. the Mutazilite theologians in Iraq argued for the reality of free will, on the grounds that God would otherwise be unjust in punishing men for wickedness, and that God could will only what was for man's good. But the implications of this latter argument, namely that man's good actually required free will, were not taken very far in Islamic thought.

THE FREE WILL DEFENCE

We now proceed to examine the free will argument irrespective of its context in a particular religion. The fact that it has been developed largely in a Christian context is irrelevant to its logic as an element in theodicy. Any monotheistic faith could use this argument, and so has an interest in the question of its validity.

The free will defence has been the subject of a great deal of discussion in recent philosophy of religion. Several philosophers have argued that it does not work. The discussion can be summarized in the form of a dialogue between an unbeliever and a believer.

UNBELIEVER You say that God is both omnipotent and perfectly good. If so, there ought not to be any evil in the world, since your God would both be able to prevent it and want to prevent it. But there is evil in the world; so either there is no God, or he is not omnipotent, or he is not perfectly good.

BELIEVER That argument looks plausible only at first sight. If God had a good reason for permitting some evil in his world, then the existence of that evil would not contradict his goodness or omnipotence.

UNBELIEVER But what on earth could count as a good reason for an omnipotent and perfectly good God to permit any evil in the world?

BELIEVER Well, suppose he wanted to create a world of persons relating lovingly and creatively to each other and to himself. Now such personal relations are inseparable from moral goodness, and moral goodness involves choice. You can't predetermine goodness or personal relations. The difference between a world of puppets and a world of persons is that persons must be genuinely free. Not even an omnipotent being can create a world of persons who are bound always to act well. It's logically impossible.

UNBELIEVER   Wait a minute. Are you sure it's logically impossible? I grant you that a world of puppets controlled externally by strings would not be a world of persons in relation. But suppose it were just built into people's natures that they always acted well in relation to each other. There's not external constraint there. They would be relating freely, but their nature would be such that they never did each other wrong or turned away from God.

BELIEVER   No. That argument won't do. I don't think you've understood what freedom is if you think that possible. Programming a creature so that he always acts well is just as much a denial of freedom as pulling strings. It would give only an illusion of freedom, like a man acting under hypnosis. Freedom is a matter of really being in control of what you do. It has to be up to you whether you respond to other people and to God lovingly and creatively. So if God is to create a world of persons he *must* allow them freedom and hence the possibility of wrong choice.

UNBELIEVER   But maybe we don't have that sort of freedom anyway. After all, modern science suggests very strongly that at least at levels above the submicroscopic every event has a cause. What's more, genetics, psychology and sociology are showing more and more how people's behaviour depends on their heredity and environment.

BELIEVER   We mustn't get sidetracked too far into philosophical debate about determinism. All I'll say to that is that I'm not arguing for absolute spontaneity. The causal factors you mention are undoubtedly there, and they certainly limit our freedom, though they also provide the material and possibilities for the exercise of our freedom. But I am prepared to say that, whatever science will discover, we know that we are able to choose between alternatives, and act in a variety of ways. In our relations with each other we know that we can act well or badly. But it's not just a matter of moral freedom. We know we can think freely too, survey different lines of argument, pick out the valid from the invalid, and judge between different proposals. If you were right, all this too, including our present argument, would be just automatic stimulus and response.

UNBELIEVER Well, we are getting sidetracked. Your claim about whatever science will discover strikes me as pretty rash. But I won't press you on that now. Let's get back to the philosophy of religion. Suppose I were to allow you your understanding of freedom and agree that it could not be predetermined that people always act well. But do you not agree that it is logically possible for a world to exist where, as a matter of fact, people always did use their freedom to act well, and as a matter of fact never did wrong.

BELIEVER I can't deny that such a world is logically possible.

UNBELIEVER Well then, if God is omnipotent, he could surely have created such a world.

BELIEVER No. That won't work either. It may be logically possible that such a world exists, but it's not logically possible that God could bring it about that things turned out like that. You can't cause it to be the case that people as a matter of fact always act well, since that matter of fact depends on them, if they're free. The logical possibility of everybody acting well is the possibility that men may themselves choose to act well, not that God may cause them to act well.

UNBELIEVER In other words you are saying that every possible world, if it is to contain persons in relation, must contain the real possibility of wrong action.

BELIEVER Yes, that's the free will defence, when it's combined with the claim that a world of persons in relation is a very good thing, and well worth creating.

UNBELIEVER At such a cost? Remember Auschwitz.

BELIEVER Ah, well, there perhaps you have me. I sometimes wonder about that myself.

UNBELIEVER Well, I won't pursue that question now. But I've thought of another difficulty with your view. Surely the free will defence as you have expounded it implies a most implausible picture of the relation between God and his creatures. Have you not made God's personal creatures so independent of their creator that he is bound to lose control of his creation? I thought that a monotheistic faith involved the belief that God not only holds every finite creature in being, but actualizes every event that takes place. Does not Aquinas say that God works in us through our will? In fact, isn't the classical view of God's sovereignty over man, in Jewish, Christian and Muslim thought, not unlike the view I myself put forward at the beginning of our discussion, whereby God might be expected to work in us a hidden way to bring it about that we do good?

BELIEVER How intriguing to find you turning into a theologian! I see your point. All I can say is that much traditional theology has not taken human freedom seriously enough. That goes for Augustine, Aquinas, Luther and Calvin. I would argue that to give creatures the power of free response to each other and to himself is indeed an act of self-limitation on the part of God. I believe that God remains omnipotent and sovereign in the sense that he knows what to do, whatever his creatures do, and that he will bring good out of evil in the end, whatever they do. But I cannot agree that it makes sense to say that God himself is, ultimately speaking, doing what his creatures are doing, if he has really given them freedom. Certainly he preserves them in being and comes to meet them and help them in many different ways, but if they are to be genuinely persons, he has to give them some degree of independence.

UNBELIEVER I've got another theological question. What about Jesus Christ? I thought Christians held that he was tempted like the rest of us, but remained quite sinless, always acting well. If a perfect human life was possible in his case, why not in everybody's case? Or wasn't he really free, in the sense you have been arguing for?

BELIEVER   That's a problem only for Christians. It wouldn't affect the use of the free will defence by other monotheists. As for Christians, I suppose they would have to say that Jesus was capable of doing wrong, but didn't, because he was so close to God in the unique relation known as Incarnation. For other men, getting close to God, or being drawn close to God is a much more arduous affair, not in the sense of our temptations being greater, but in the sense that we start off so much further from God, and have to be drawn into relation with him.

UNBELIEVER   That sounds highly obscure, but since its a special Christian difficulty, let's leave it on one side and come back to the free will defence in general. From what you've said, it sounds to me as if, on your view, all possible worlds containing persons must not only contain the possibility of wrong action, but also a very great deal of actual evil.

BELIEVER   You may be right. The theoretical possibility of everybody as a matter of fact acting well may be there in the beginning, but the vast probability is that any world containing persons will at some stage go wrong, especially if there are good reasons for them to be rooted in a physical environment at some distance from God.

UNBELIEVER   What's that? You've slipped in a large new point there, haven't you?

BELIEVER   Well, yes, I have. I admit that I'm now thinking of physical suffering or natural evil, as well as moral evil resulting from the conditions of free choice. Perhaps we ought not to get on to that until we resume our discussion in the next chapter.

IVAN'S QUESTION

This imaginary discussion has shown something of the force of the free will defence in the context of theistic religion. But one of its weak points, where the believer seemed most ill at ease, was over the question of the cost of creating a world of persons in relation. This was precisely Ivan Karamazov's point, when he urged that it was not worth creating a world of life and beauty and personal relations, if it necessarily cost the suffering of one innocent creature. It was this consideration that made him return his entrance ticket.

Moreover, as the unbeliever pointed out in the discussion, it is not just a matter of the suffering of one innocent creature. It is the immense amount of suffering due to human wickedness in countless cases throughout history. In talking about the necessary risk of the abuse of freedom if there is to be a world of persons in relation, we have to remember that we are talking about the risk of Hitler's or Stalin's concentration camps, the torture and extermination of millions of people in the twentieth century alone. It is not surprising that the believer's confidence faltered at that stage in the discussion.

There are two possible lines of argument which might be developed in reply to Ivan's question. In the first place, the believer would have to try to show that the good of creation, including its ultimate destiny, outweighed the evil caused by the abuse of human freedom. This would be a very difficult task if the unbeliever refused to allow any talk of human destiny, and restricted attention to this present world order, although something could be said about the beauties and values already realized in past and present. Equally, something could be said about the possibilities of courage, sympathy, forgiveness and the creative use of suffering, virtues consequent upon the fact of suffering and already mentioned in our survey of the ways of coping with evil and suffering. But the horrors of perversion and cruelty are so numerous and so appalling that, unless the believer were allowed to refer to the transcendent goal of the creative process, where, to quote the book of Revelation, 'God shall wipe away every tear from their eye', his insistence that the greater good of creation not only outweighs those evils but makes the risk of them worthwhile is likely to have a very hollow ring.

In one respect Ivan is perhaps unfair in the way he puts the dilemma. He asks Alyosha if he would be prepared to create 'a fabric of human destiny with the object of making men happy in

65

the end, giving them peace and rest at the last', if 'it was essential and inevitable to torture to death only one tiny creature'. And Alyosha can only say, 'No, I wouldn't consent'. But the theistic view of creation does not, if the free will defence is valid, involve attributing the evils directly to God's action. God certainly allows their possibility, even the very high probability of their actuality, but the direct responsibility for wrong action has to be attributed to those who abuse freedom by failing to act well.

A second line of argument open to the believer is this: Ivan's argument implies that the creation of a world of persons in relation is not worth the risk of the evils which it makes possible. Better no creation at all than the risk of any innocent suffering, let alone that of the scale of Auschwitz. But if we took this argument absolutely seriously we could never justify having children. For we too bring into being a world of persons, our own children, and we do so in the full knowledge of the possibilities for evil as well as for good which obtain in the world. No doubt many children are brought into the world irresponsibly and thoughtlessly, but some parents, at least, think carefully about having a family, and if Ivan's moral argument were valid, they would never be justified in going ahead. Nevertheless we do have children, in the faith and confidence that the good of life outweighs the risks and possibilities of disaster.

The main difficulty with this line of argument is that whereas human parents are mercifully ignorant of what their children are going to do and of what will happen to them, and so can go ahead and have a family in the hope that things will go well with them, God, it is usually believed, knows what will happen, and although he does not directly bring about his creatures' misdeeds, his omniscience precludes that happy state of ignorance which characterizes human parenthood. This consideration places the believer in a very problematic position. He can argue, somewhat dubiously in many theologians' opinion, that not even omniscience knows the future, since the future, being open, does not yet exist and so is not there to be known. On this view it is simply a mistake to think of past, present and future being equally present to the eternal divine mind. Rather the creation of a temporal world means the creation of energies and structures with potentialities yet to be realized in a number of possible ways. So while God knows precisely what is possible for his creatures, as well as knowing precisely what he will do about whatever they do, nevertheless he does not know precisely what they will do until they do it. On this view God's self-limitation in the creation of a temporal world goes further than many have supposed.

It is, incidentally the widespread conviction of God's omniscience that makes it difficult for the believer to hold to the distinction between divine causality and divine permission, which is so important for the free will defence. If these speculations about the necessary self-limitation in the divine knowledge consequent upon the creation of a temporally structured world have any force, then it is that much easier to uphold the notion of divine permission. Even if not, it probably remains the case that anyone who takes human freedom seriously will be justified in appealing to the distinction between what God brings about and what God allows.

Whatever the rights and wrongs of this dispute, the Christian believer will certainly want to admit that a morally acceptable view of creation requires men to suppose that God takes ultimate responsibility for his creation, even though he is not immediately responsible for what his free creatures do. It has been a central tenet of Christianity that God does take that responsibility upon himself by entering the structures of his creation and bearing the brunt of the world's evil himself to the point of crucifixion.

5

PHYSICAL SUFFERING AND THE
NATURE OF THE PHYSICAL WORLD

Even if successful the free will defence explains only some of
the world's evils: the facts of wrong choice and human wickedness both individual and communal. As was pointed out earlier,
this does not explain the presence and frequency of natural disasters, diseases and accidents in the world. And it only partly
explains the suffering actually caused by human wickedness,
for example, by a protracted and cruel war such as the world
wars of our century or the war in Vietnam. Granted that these
evils are brought about by human action, it remains the case that
it is the nature of the physical world and the structure of conscious and sentient beings such as ourselves that render the
consequences of evil actions so terrible. Part of the problem
of evil is the fact that, the structure of our bodies, nerves and
brains being what it is, physical and mental torture (as well as
disease and accident) can take such horrific forms.

Theodicy, therefore, is bound to include consideration of the
nature and role of the physical world, and of physical and mental
pain.

THE AMBIGUITIES OF THE NATURAL WORLD

It is an extraordinary thing that this same natural world can
present such different appearances to its inhabitants, in ordinary
life, in art, in philosophy and in religion. In ordinary life people
can be struck again and again by its wonders and beauties—trees,
mountains, lakes and stars, the supple grace of animals, the
tenderness of human love; they can also be struck by the alien
indifference of impersonal forces, by 'nature red in tooth and
claw', by boredom, by the malice of others, by fear of madness

or just senility. In art we find on the one side the beauties of landscape painting, nature poetry, harmonious music, cathedral, mosque and temple architecture, on the other side the literature of despair, the screaming paintings of Roger Bacon and the theatre of the absurd. In philosophy we have the conviction of Leibniz that this is 'the best of all possible worlds', while others, like Sartre, present us with a world of anguish and alienation, or follow Ivan Karamazov in returning their entrance ticket.

In religion, too, the range of different evaluations of the natural world is very great. We have, in the course of our survey of religious responses to the facts of evil, come across interpretations of the world as illusion, as suffering, as the divine dance or play, as an ever-recurrent cyclical process of growth and decay, as fallen from an original state of perfection and given over to the devil's dominion, as an unfinished goal-directed process, consisting in the creative fashioning of a context of life and personal growth and love. One big difference between the world religions is over the status of the natural world as creation; we have noted that the problem of evil looms largest where the world is seen as wholly dependent for its being and nature on the creative will of an omnipotent and benevolent deity.

The idea that the world is the creation of an infinite all-powerful God was not easily achieved. Ancient religions and cosmologies often thought of the creator as a limited being. In Plato's *Timaeus*, for example, the divine architect (the 'demiurge') was limited both by the eternal forms, in accordance with which he designed the world, and by the pre-existent matter out of which he shaped it. Later Platonism moved away from these views. The forms came to be thought of as ideas in the divine mind, and it was held that all levels of being proceed by emanation from the One right down to the level of matter. The development of Christian doctrine was greatly influenced by this later Platonism, and shared its rejection of all dualistic notions. For Augustine every substance was God's good creation. In such Christian thought, moreover, the theory of emanation was firmly rejected, and the natural world was seen as having been brought into being out of nothing by God through a sheer act of will. That is why evil is such a serious problem for Christian thought.

69

The details of ancient cosmologies need not concern us here. But the idea that certain necessities impose themselves upon the creator is not finally dismissed with the rejection of dualism. Monotheism may come to reject the notion that there are external necessities limiting the creator, but the creator's omnipotence cannot be thought of as putting him outside the scope of internal logical necessities. Not even God could do something self-contradictory. We have seen this already in the case of freedom. It may be that the creation of a world of persons imposes further logical constraints upon the creator than we have so far allowed.

What we have to investigate is the suggestion that physical suffering, too, results from certain logically necessary structures in creation.

THE PROBLEM OF PHYSICAL SUFFERING

The main question, then, for the believer, in respect of physical evil, is this: why did God create a natural order endowed with such properties and powers as to make possible the pains and accidents and damage which in fact afflict his creatures?

First, however, we need some further explanation why the view that physical evil is caused by the devil's interference is not taken seriously here. Of course, if that were the case, then the believer would after all be able to place the whole weight of theodicy on the free will defence; for the devil, as a fallen angel, would be one more example of a free creature gone to the bad. And all suffering, including that of natural disaster, accident, disease and death, could then be attributed to the misuse of free will. There are Christian philosophers who hold this view, or at least regard its logical possibility as a sufficient basis for theodicy. But it is open to two grave objections. In the first place, it is extremely difficult to make theological sense of this supposition. As has been pointed out before, the picture of a God who permits his creation to fall into the grip of a supernatural irredeemable malicious spiritual agent is not a religiously or theologically plausible picture. It is quite understandable, given the history of religion from its earliest beginnings, that such an idea should have been developed out of primitive animistic and demonological views, but as soon as theological rationality seeks to spell out a developed and consistent view of God, man and the world, the mythological nature of such personifications of evil tends to become apparent. Consequently the Christian theologian today is likely to treat the devil as a symbolic figure and thus to abandon any explanatory function which the devil may once have had regarding physical evil.

In the second place modern scientific knowledge of the basic energies and structures of the physical universe, incomplete and fragmentary as it is, nevertheless makes it extremely difficult to suppose that the physical world might have had different and less harmful properties, had it not been interfered with by the devil. There is great implausibility in the notion that science is investigating not the structures of creation, but the structures of a twisted and perverted physical universe.

These theological and scientific implausibilities combine to dispose the modern theist to reject this kind of appeal to the devil.

Hints of an alternative solution to the problem can be gathered from two older treatments of the question of pain, one from the Jewish and one from the Christian tradition. The name of the medieval Jewish philosopher, Moses Maimonides (A.D. 1135–1204), has already been mentioned in connection with the free will defence (p. 57). It is interesting, however, to observe that in *The Guide of the Perplexed* he also considers the evils which befall man through possession of a body. He points out that all bodily corruption is a consequence of the changeable matter out of which self-reproducing creatures are made rather than the forms into which they are made. But, he argues, these particular forms could not exist without matter, so 'it was necessary that man's very noble form ... should be bound to earthy, turbid, and dark matter'. (Bk III, ch. 8.) Maimonides does not regard matter as something uncreated, imposing these necessities upon God from outside. Still less does he regard matter as evil; for everything God creates is good. On the contrary God creates matter in order that there shall be self-reproducing creatures. According to Maimonides these are not the only personal creatures that there are, but it is a good thing that there should be self-

71

reproducing creatures as well as other kinds. Now 'were it not for the passing away of the individuals, the coming-to-be relating to the species would not continue'. He quotes the ancient writer Galen as having said: 'Do not set your mind on the vain thought that it is possible that out of menstrual blood and sperm there should be generated a living being that does not die, is not subject to pain, is in perpetual motion, or is as brilliant as the sun'. In other words Maimonides is beginning to explore the idea that the very creation of a world of organic, self-reproducing creatures imposes certain necessary conditions on its creator. He does not explore these arguments very far, and he is prevented from realizing their full weight by his belief that the whole creation contains many other creatures such as angels, unencumbered by these necessities. Consequently he would not be able to rebut the counter-argument that since other purely spiritual personal beings can quite easily be created, the creation of self-reproducing personal beings rooted in a material world is hardly worth the cost in suffering. Again, although Maimonides also speaks of matter as a veil between God and the human intellect, he does not suggest that some such veil is necessary if any personal creature is to have some relative independence of being from his creator. A third limitation in Maimonides' theodicy is the fact that he is over-optimistic about the rarity of physical evil in the world, and its small place in relation to the whole of God's creation. This latter suggestion has always been one of the most implausible arguments in any religious tradition.

When we turn to the medieval Christian philosopher Thomas Aquinas, we find a mind of truly astonishing breadth and precision. The modern Christian theologian can by no means follow him in every argument, and we have already had reason to note some criticism of his views on God's control of men's free acts. But his treatment of God's will and providence in the *Summa Theologiae* (1a. 19–26) includes a number of observations which indicate his awareness of the conditions which, by his decision to create an ordered universe, God necessarily imposes upon himself.

Aquinas' basic principle regarding evil has already been quoted: God 'permits certain defects in particular effects, that the perfect good of the universe may not be hindered'. The point is that the good of the whole universe necessarily implies the possibility of some evil. Now Aquinas does not only apply this principle to the case of free will and moral evil. Where physical evil is concerned, he says that God wills it only in the sense of willing the good to which it is attached; for example 'willing to maintain the balance of nature', God 'wills that some things should follow their constitutional course and die away'. This involves Aquinas once again in the important distinction between what God wills directly and what he wills indirectly or only permits. The good of the whole is willed directly, the concomitant evils, if such there be, are willed only indirectly. The point of the argument is to show that God could not have the one without the other.

To put the matter in modern terminology, it is logically impossible to will the balance of nature without willing the death of individuals. Aquinas was clear about the implications of this: 'anything that implies a contradiction does not fall under God's omnipotence'. God can no more create a balance of nature without the death of individuals than he can create a square circle.

This brief examination of Maimonides and Aquinas has yielded the insight that there may well be logically necessary conditions which make it impossible to create an ordered physical universe containing organic creatures without the possibility of accident and pain. This line of argument can be reinforced by our increased scientific knowledge of the laws of nature and the structure of the physical and chemical components of the natural world. For we have come to see more clearly that it is the operation of the same general laws that both has led to the evolution of sentient and conscious life, with all its possibilities for good and creativity, and also makes inevitable the kind of accident and damage and pain which constitute the problem of physical evil. To wish away the evils is to wish away the conditions of all life and growth as well. Consequently the more we know about the structure and interconnectedness of the physical universe, the less easily can we imagine alternative universes which retain the good features of ours, but lack the bad.

But now the theodicist has to ask himself the question which arose in the case of Maimonides' and Aquinas' arguments. Granted that the creation of a world of self-reproducing creatures with a built-in natural balance imposes upon the creator certain necessary conditions which make for evil as well as for good, why create such a universe at all? The most powerful reply to this question would, it seems, be to say that some such universe is the necessary condition not only of the actual goods of human personal existence, as we know them, but of any personal existence over against the creator at all. This was the argument that Maimonides was not in a position to deploy.

Can such an argument be produced? An intimation of such a view is to be found in the writings of Professor John Hick on the problem of evil. He introduces the notion of what he calls the 'epistemic distance' between human beings and their creator. In order to have a certain relative independence of being and knowledge from their creator, created persons must have, as it were, a footing in reality at a distance from the creator, and if they are to be genuinely free and individual selves, their knowledge of God must be indirectly, even arduously, acquired, rather than thrust upon them from the beginning. The personal being of creatures, in other words, necessarily requires some such kind of context as is provided by a material evolving universe, which builds up from the simplest energies an ordered environment for personal life and growth. Personal beings, so constructed, have the chance, in such an environment, to be themselves before being wooed or called into relation with their maker. The physical world is indeed a veil between God and his creatures, as Maimonides says, but such a veil has a necessary function in the economy of creation. Without it, there could not really be finite persons at all. The idea of a world of purely spiritual created beings, or the idea of heaven created directly without the prior process of the nurturing of persons in a relatively independent cosmos, would on this view be impossible ideas.

It is not just a question of God's providing his creatures with the necessary conditions of moral growth and character. That, as has already been argued, would give us a somewhat over-moralistic view of the universe. The veil of the evolving material

74

creation is not so much a necessary condition of moral character as a necessary condition of finite personal being as such. Only if rooted in an environment at a distance from the creator can persons come to be at all. Once established in being as free persons they can then be drawn into relation with their maker and perhaps immortalized. Once they have acquired their self-hood by this means, they can become the objects of whatever future God has in store for them. Creation in and through some such process as an evolving material universe is, on this view, not one possible way of creating a world among others. It is the only possible way. This is a large claim. But, if true, its explanatory power is great. The evils men experience from their physical structure and environment are not just by-products of a created order which is the necessary condition for particular goods which they experience; they are by-products of a process which is the necessary condition for their being created finite persons at all.

Such an argument concerning physical evil bears a close analogy to the free will defence concerning moral evil. Just as personal being requires freedom and therefore the possibility of wrong choice, so does finite free personal being require an ordered yet flexible physical environment in which to be rooted and nurtured over against and at a certain distance from the creator. Such an environment cannot preclude the possibility of accident and physical harm.

THE DIALOGUE RESUMED

Let us once again summarise the argument in the form of further dialogue between the unbeliever and the believer.

UNBELIEVER   We talked before about the evils of human wicked-ness, and you tried to convince me that the gift of freedom, as you call it, explains their presence in the world. You also argued that freedom is a necessary condition of personal being, so that if God wanted to create a world of persons, he had to give them free will. Suppose I were to agree with you on that point (which I don't), you still haven't begun to explain the physical evil which besets mankind, the pain and loss and torture and

75

maiming which people suffer, sometimes through human action, sometimes through natural disasters like earthquakes, famines or floods.

BELIEVER I admit that. But there are things to be said on that score too. In the first place, you can surely see that, given a physical world as the theatre of organic life, pain has a necessary function for sentient and conscious beings. It is a necessary warning system, and a stimulus against danger, unnoticed disease and the neglect of essential needs. On a purely natural view, animal and human sensitivity to pain would not have evolved if it did not have an important role to play in the survival of species and individuals.

UNBELIEVER That's hardly a theological argument. And wouldn't some other system, say, the withdrawal of pleasurable sensations have done just as well?

BELIEVER I doubt it. I doubt if creatures insensitive to pain would react quickly enough; and there is evidence that human beings born with faulty nervous systems succumb very quickly to unnoticed disease or accident. Anyway, you neglect two other facts, one, that some pains and losses, those accompanying old age and death, for instance, are inevitable in a world of organic self-reproducing creatures, with its complicated interrelated ecology, and, two, that the structures of physical life which give rise to the pains you're complaining about are also the source of all the joys and excellences of human sensitivity and awareness. I don't see how you can have one without the other.

UNBELIEVER The trouble with your arguments is that you begin by accepting the physical organic world and then try to see how it makes sense and all hangs together. My point is that I can't see why your God should create such a universe in the first place, if it would necessarily involve such suffering for his creatures. Why not create an entirely different kind of world, a perfect world, such as you yourself envisage heaven to be? Why go through all the palaver of the past and present evolutionary process?

BELIEVER I should want to answer that at several different

levels. I should, for one thing, want to repeat what I've just said about the excellences of bodily existence, the beauties of nature, and all the exquisite things and experiences extolled in poetry, art and music. If they are all aspects of a natural world with a given structure and laws of development, you cannot isolate them from the less happy side-effects of that same structure of interacting systems. Then, secondly, you need to reckon with the way in which the evils you complain of are not all pure loss. There are features of human excellence—courage, sympathy, sacrificial love, which can supervene upon the ills of human life ...

UNBELIEVER Wait. You've just said something quite intolerable, morally speaking. You can't possibly be arguing that suffering is justified because of the sympathy it evokes?

BELIEVER No, no, I didn't say that and I didn't mean it. I could not for one moment use that argument to explain the presence of suffering. All I was saying was that, given the existence of suffering, there are, at least sometimes, creative ways of coping with it. I'm not saying that that explains anything. The explanation comes in at a much more general level, when we see that pain and accident and loss are inevitable aspects of an evolving organic world.

UNBELIEVER But then let me press my basic question again. Why embark on such a costly process?

BELIEVER Well, I suppose my fundamental answer to that is that only in some such context or environment can a world of finite persons, that is to say genuinely autonomous agents, come into being at all separately from their divine creator. God has to give them a base, so to speak, in a relatively independent and law-governed world. Otherwise they would have no freedom and individuality of their own.

UNBELIEVER That seems an unlikely hypothesis. What about the angels?

BELIEVER If the argument about a *necessary* veil between creator and creature is valid, then angels are impossible.

77

UNBELIEVER Oh, really? Your theodicy is beginning to have some rather odd consequences from the point of view of orthodoxy.

BELIEVER I find it odd that you should once again appear to have a vested interest in orthodoxy.

UNBELIEVER Well, let that pass. Let's suppose that some such context or environment is necessary, as you suggest. Why is it such a botched job? What are earthquakes doing here? Couldn't the system have been expected to run more smoothly?

BELIEVER You seem to have got hold of a false model. I'm not talking about the universe as a single great machine. That would never have produced persons. Only a flexible organism evolving from a host of mutually interacting systems, combining law-governed processes with genuine spontaneity, can be the vehicle of finite free and personal life and thought. But such a process and such creatures are bound to be at risk to accidental clashes, at the different levels of created being—atomic, molecular, organic and so on. Nevertheless, it is some such process as this which is the necessary condition of finite personal being.

UNBELIEVER I find it difficult to follow your treatment of the role of the creator in all this. He seems to be disappearing from view behind the laws and structures you are postulating as necessary.

BELIEVER Well, I do think that, if the physical creation is to do its job as an initially independent context and environment for personal life and growth, then there is a sense in which the hand of the creator must be hidden, and the creation must be an indirect process in and through material agencies and energies each with their own God-given powers. As one writer has said, 'God makes the creature make itself'. The higher levels of creation are evolved out of the interaction of lower level energies, each following its own law-governed nature, without any faking or forcing by direct unmediated intervention. That is why there are sometimes accidental clashes at lower levels, as when a cerebral haemorrhage occurs. But this is an unhappy by-product of the same laws of molecular and organic functioning which for the most part carry and foster the working of the brain and the thinking it makes possible. The haemorrhage is not a direct act of God. God, we might say, wills complex wholes like the brain to exist and function harmoniously, but creates them indirectly by creating fundamental particles with the power to combine, through evolution, in such a way as to constitute the brains of organisms. The indirect method makes possible free and relatively independent personal creatures, rooted in a material environment. However, it necessarily involves as well the possibility of accidental malfunctioning at the various lower levels (and of course accidents at the level of everyday experience as when a man falls off a cliff or a motor accident takes place).

UNBELIEVER This sounds a pretty austere sort of theodicy to me. I notice that you talk once again of freedom. Just as in the last chapter you said that free will was the necessary condition of personal life and growth, now you say that some such ordered yet flexible structure of interacting systems as we find in this physical universe is the necessary condition of the evolution of free persons over against God.

BELIEVER Yes. Freedom comes in at this point too.

UNBELIEVER I'm not sure that I find that any more plausible than the view which blames it all on the devil.

THE BEST OF ALL POSSIBLE WORLDS?

The seventeenth century German rationalist philosopher Leibniz believed that this is the best of all possible worlds, and necessarily so, since there could be no possible reason why God should have created anything but the best. This view was ridiculed by Voltaire in his play *Candide*, in the face of such appalling evils as the Lisbon earthquake of 1755. Empiricist philosophers such as David Hume thought it only too easy to suggest ways in which God might have created a much better world. He might have limited the excessive powers of nature, or enhanced the weak powers of man; or he might not have left things to the operation of general laws, but rather intervened surreptitiously from time-to-time to prevent disasters and accidents. But this reaction against Leibniz' picture of things being necessarily what they are is perhaps too hasty. If our previous arguments about the interconnectedness of things are right, it is by no means so easy to suggest such improvements in the ordering of the world. They would undoubtedly have undesirable repercussions elsewhere, or else they would involve the sort of direct interference by God which would belie the role of the created universe as a necessary veil between God and man, providing the required 'epistemic distance' for men to become autonomous and responsible agents.

This is not to go back to Leibniz. The best of all possible worlds is not a coherent notion in respect of a finite universe containing genuine contingency and having a genuinely open future. Not all things in this world are interrelated by bonds of necessity. But it does make sense to suggest that *some such* world as this is the necessary condition of the creation of persons, and so to that extent that this world is *a* best possible world, despite its inevitable evils. Moreover, when we make so bold as to evaluate the whole universe in this way, it is no use thinking of it just as it is at present. If the creation is, necessarily, a process whereby persons acquire their selfhood and character, in order to be immortalized by God in a perfected future state, then it is the whole process, including its end-state, which we are evaluating as *a* best possible world.

It is not easy to pinpoint the notion of necessity involved in the idea that *some such* world as this is a necessary condition of the creation of persons. To hold this view would not be to say that every actual evil is necessary. Far from it. Many actual evils could have been prevented, but many could not have even been predicted, being purely contingent upon independent processes coming into chance conflict. All one would be saying would be that, given the necessity of some such law-governed universe as this, then some such evils will necessarily occur. Equally, however, without some such structure, the good of creation, and especially the good of a finite world of personal being, would have been impossible.

Precisely the same question, whether such a costly process is worthwhile, recurs at the end of our discussion of the necessary role of the physical world as occurred at the end of our discussion of the free will defence. Ivan Karamazov's rejection of God's world as too costly may again be the instinctive reaction of morally sensitive people.

The believer will deploy the same arguments in reply, referring to the greater preponderance of good over evil, when the whole process of creation including its future goal is taken into consideration, to the distinction between what God wills and what God permits, and if he is a Christian believer, to the way of the Cross, by which God takes responsibility for the world's evil, by embracing it himself. There is perhaps a further point which the believer might make in reply to Ivan. If the arguments of the present chapter have any force, then he can point to the fact that there really is no other way in which God could have given us being and life than by rooting us in some such structured open world as this. To return one's entrance ticket is to opt for no created world at all. That may in fact be what Ivan Karamazov is doing. It is an understandable if sad reaction. Its moral justification, however, is perhaps not quite so obvious as he implies, if it can be shown that no radically alternative world can exist.

6

DIVINE PROVIDENCE

The theodicy which has been explored in the last two chapters requires the believer to suppose that, in creating a world of persons to exist and grow in relation to each other and to himself, God necessarily placed them in an ordered yet flexible environment, the context both of relatively independent being and of free action. The spatio-temporal evolving cosmos as we know it is not itself necessary for the purpose. But *some such* world is the necessary condition of finite personal life, and the actual world in fact fulfils this dual role of providing on the one hand a screen or veil between creator and creature, and on the other a reliable environment for freedom and growth. This view of the world constitutes a theodicy in that it explains the presence in the world of both moral evil and physical suffering, the former being an inevitable possibility if freedom is to be real, the latter being an inevitable by-product of a cosmos flexible yet ordered enough to evolve self-reproducing persons (some such cosmos being the necessary condition of *any* created personal life).

Such a theodicy, however, raises grave problems for the theist over the notion of divine providence. It appears to be a form of deism, a religious philosophy popular in the eighteenth century, according to which God was believed to have created the physical universe, but to have left it to operate by itself in accordance with the laws he gave it. Traditional theism, by contrast, has usually taught that God is active in the world, caring for his individual creatures, and bringing about his particular purposes within and for the created world. This is what the doctrine of divine providence means. Belief in providence is, on any reckoning, hard to sustain in face of the world's evil; but the theodicy under consideration might appear to have been bought only at the price of abandoning the notion of providence and resorting to a kind of deism.

In this chapter, therefore, we examine the different ways in which divine providence has been understood, in order to see if there exists an acceptable view which might enable the theist on the one hand to hold on to his explanation of evil in terms of the necessary conditions of free personal being, and on the other hand to affirm his belief in God's providential care for individuals and for the world.

IDEAS OF PROVIDENCE IN TRIBAL AND ANCIENT RELIGIONS

In tribal religions the notion of divine providence is common. It appears in several different forms. At one level the natural phenomena which generally sustain life are regarded as God's provision for men. Rain and sunshine symbolize his benevolence. Among many African tribes God is known as 'the Rain Giver'. He is thought of as a shepherd protecting his flock, or 'carrying' his children as a mother carries her baby on her back. Healing from sickness is widely attributed to God's providential care.

In the religions of Greece and Rome the gods were certainly thought of as active in human affairs, and Athene was worshipped at Delphi under the name *Pronoia*, which means 'forethought' and is the standard Greek word for providence. But, as has been already pointed out, more impersonal notions came to prevail, and the gods themselves were held to be subject to fate or necessity. However, it is in Stoicism that we find the widest discussion of providence in the ancient world, although it is a very different notion of providence from that of personal, fatherly care. According to the Stoics divine providence is the orderly system of nature, permeated by divine harmony and reason. Thus to live in accordance with nature is to live by divine providence, since God orders all things for the best. For the Stoic 'fate' and 'providence' mean much the same thing.

The difficulty with the tribal religions' view of providence is precisely the problem of evil. Unsystematic religious thinking tends to treat particular beneficial events as providential while ignoring particular harmful events. Alternatively, the harmful events may also be explained as intended, either by malicious agents, or by God as punishment or trial. But the reflective religious mind finds increasing difficulty in the notion that every event is the result of a particular intentional act. The Stoic view, however, has the opposite difficulty. When everything is felt to proceed by divinely established general laws, everything that happens tends to be experienced as necessary, and so the only appropriate response is resignation. We shall see that these two opposite extremes represent recurring tendencies in the history of religious ideas of providence.

EASTERN IDEAS OF PROVIDENCE

The notion of *karma-samsāra*, so pervasive in Indian thought, might appear to militate against the development of ideas of personal providence. If the universal law of moral cause and effect determines the fate of individuals in an endless round of birth and rebirth, then there is little scope for the idea of the providential guidance of history towards an ultimate goal. In its devotional forms, however, Hinduism developed ideas of God as supervising the operation of *karma* and annulling its effects on behalf of his devotees. Divine providence is also at work in the Avatārs, in whom God is held to manifest himself in incarnate form whenever there is especially grievous need in the world. The dispute already mentioned between the 'monkey' school and the 'cat' school among the followers of Rāmānuja shows that a vivid sense of the operation of the divine grace in the individual believer could be stimulated by devotional Hinduism. But there is nothing in the Hindu tradition to correspond to the conviction of divine providence in natural evolution and in universal history, such as we find in the Judaeo-Christian tradition.

Buddhism is even less hospitable to the notion of providence. There is a sense in which the appearances of the Buddha were regarded as providential. In the Buddhist myths the whole earth responded to the Buddha's enlightenment as the crucial event which makes the way of salvation possible for men, and the Bodhisattva doctrines of Mahāyāna Buddhism reintroduce notions of grace absent from the earlier tradition. Rejection of belief in a supreme creator God, however, prevented the Buddhists from acquiring any real apprehension of the world and human life as being under divine providential care.

In his book *Myths, Dreams and Mysteries* (Fontana), Mircea Eliade points out how widespread in the history of religions are the conceptions of mythical time and of the eternal return—the notion, that is, of the cosmos passing through recurrent phases of development and decline. These ideas are not peculiar to Indian religion, although they are prominent in the Hindu and Buddhist myths as well as in the common notion of *karma-samsāra*; but it remains true that India has been particularly hospitable to such pervasive beliefs. Eliade goes on to stress the revolutionary nature, in the history of religions, of the Jewish idea of a particular providence in history, of Yahweh's intervention in history and formation of a particular future-orientated path through history. It is in this soil that the notion of providence has flourished.

IDEAS OF PROVIDENCE IN THE DEVELOPED THEISTIC RELIGIONS

The idea of a chosen people with a historical vocation to manifest the true nature of God to the world, coupled with a conception of history as moving under God towards a final and ultimate consummation, is the legacy of Israel to the whole Judaeo-Christian tradition, and is, as Mircea Eliade realized, a decisively new conception in world religion.

It was the fundamental belief of ancient Israel that through Abraham, Moses and the prophets Yahweh was fashioning for himself in human history a people to whom he had bound himself by covenant and who were to be the vehicle of his self-revelation to the whole world. The whole course of history, they believed, was overruled by God; for he used even the armies of the foreign nations like a rod to chastise his disobedient people. Even an unparalleled disaster like the fall of Jerusalem in 586 B.C. and the Babylonian exile could not thwart his purpose. On the contrary they were the means by which he purified a faithful remnant of his people, who would and did return to their homeland, to wait expectantly for God's Messiah and their

85

ultimate vindication. Within this framework God's providential overruling of the lives of individuals had always been clear in the lives of the prophets and kings, but it became a problematic notion in the later literature of the Hebrew Bible, as awareness of the innocent suffering of individual men and women such as Job became more and more insistent. We have examined some of the ways in which they tried to meet the problem.

Christianity took over the Jewish understanding of history as a future-orientated process under God's guidance, and saw the particular history of Israel as the preparation for the incarnation. The life, death and resurrection of Jesus came to be seen as the pivot of human history, the central point of revelation and redemption, and an anticipation of the final Kingdom of God, towards which human history is moving. Within that history a new body, the Christian Church, was now believed to be the vehicle of God's special providence in the world. Just as an expectation of final divine intervention to bring about the ultimate fulfilment of God's purpose in history had characterized the Jewish faith from the time of the exile on, so now it became a common feature of early Christian hope. But in time this hope receded to a more distant future, and a long period of church expansion came to be envisaged as part of God's providential purpose, so that the gospel might be brought to the limits of the world. Within this framework, too, belief in God's providential care of individuals was sharpened. Jesus had taught that every hair of a man's head is numbered, that every sparrow is in the hand of God, and that men need not worry about the necessities of life; for the man who seeks first God's Kingdom and righteousness will find these things provided for. Paul clearly felt his own life and mission to be under the guiding hand of God. Of course, the individual Christian did not expect to be exempt from suffering. Martyrdom and a share in Christ's suffering might be God's will for him, but in life and in death he was in God's hands, and out of martyrdom the Church would grow.

A comparable faith in divine providence is to be found in Islam. The Qur'ān speaks of God's provision for both men and animals, and, without developing so central a theology of universal history as did the Judaeo-Christian tradition, Islam has always

86

seen the role of Muhammad, the last and greatest of the prophets, as carrying to its climax the history of divine revelation. The rapid success and expansion of Islam could not but be regarded as providential. But we have already noted how, when things cease to go well for them, Muslims tend to become fatalistic and to fall back upon this faith in the inscrutable will of God. Similarly, the individual Muslim tends to see himself as in God's hands, for good or ill.

PROVIDENCE AS DIRECT DIVINE INTERVENTION

Given that western religion has developed such a strong sense of divine providence in nature, history and individual life, the question arises, how does it think that God's providential action in the world actually takes place. The simplest and most unsophisticated religious view, common in the history of Judaism, Christianity and Islam (as indeed in that of the Hindu theistic sects), is that God's providential action takes the form of miraculous intervention. The biblical tradition, like most religious traditions, is full of miracle stories, some of them, like the Exodus story, or the raising of Lazarus, quite obviously miraculous; others, like the restoration of the exiles to Jerusalem or the rapid spread of the Christian Church to the centre of the Roman world, being less obvious but just as firmly attributed to the active causality of God within the human world.

In the development of Christian faith and understanding down the centuries this way of regarding divine providence as direct causal intervention by God has come to represent one major way of thinking of divine providential activity in the world. It was this attitude that made the Catholic Christian tradition search out and collect miracle stories about the saints, and Puritan Christians in the seventeenth century encourage each other to collect accounts of 'special providences', instances where it was clear that God had intervened to protect his children. An example of the latter is the case described by John Flavel in his *Divine Conduct, or the Mystery of Providence Opened*,[1] of a soldier

[1] First published 1678. Reprinted in *The Works of John Flavel*. Banner of Truth Trust 1968.

in the seventeenth century English civil war, who was preserved, while in hiding, because a hen laid her eggs each day within reach of his hiding place. Clearly the implication is that God caused the hen to lay her eggs there. Other examples suggest that God also intervenes by putting ideas into people's heads, say in a dream. Flavel tells another story of a man who felt moved to visit a friend late at night, and found him about to hang himself.

It is this notion of providence as particular divine causal intervention in and upon the material and mental worlds that the nineteenth-century atheist philosopher Ludwig Feuerbach had in mind when he said that belief in providence is belief in miracle.

There are three main difficulties with this theory of providence as miracle. In the first place it is difficult to attribute some physical or mental event, which seems to have a perfectly natural explanation in terms of prior causes, stimuli or decisions, at one and the same time to direct divine causal activity. This problem does not arise in the case of what I called obvious miracles, if such there be, cases, that is, where there is no natural explanation. In the majority of cases, however, where God is thought of not so much as breaking the ordinary structures of creation as bending them to his purposes, it is very difficult for someone, scientifically aware of the natural energies and interactions involved, and of the general laws which they exemplify, to continue to attribute such events to the direct causal intervention of God as well. There is a sense in which scientific knowledge of the causes of events is bound to inhibit men's attributing them to the particular causal activity of a supernatural agent.

Then there are two theological difficulties. First, the direct interventionist view of divine providence seems to treat God's purposive causal activity as one causal factor among others, bringing about the things that happen in the world. This seems to reduce God to one more piece of the world, one more power at work among others. This hardly gives a credible picture either of the infinite transcendent God of theism or of the world with its created energies, powers and structures.

But the main difficulty stems from the problem of evil. If it really is God's way to intervene miraculously to bring about his purposes in nature, history and individual life, then why does he not do so more often and to greater effect? Even if the interventionist accepts the free will defence, and admits that God does not override his creatures' freedom, he still has to try to make some sense of all the physical suffering, natural disasters and accidents in the world. The theodicy explored in the last chapter involved taking seriously the role of the law-governed structures of the physical creation. But this is an argument against interventionism. The necessary role of a structured physical creation was advanced as the reason why God does not intervene.

EXISTENTIALIST AND PERSPECTIVIST VIEWS OF PROVIDENCE

The difficulties stemming from scientific knowledge, the theological implausibility of treating God as one cause among others, and the problem of evil, have combined to make many theologians in the modern world explore the possibility of a quite different understanding of what it means to speak of divine providence.

Some modern theologians, influenced by a school of continental philosophy known as existentialism (so called from its concentration on what it means to *exist* as a human being in the world), see the faith of men and women as the only point of contact between God and man. Only in and through a man's spiritual response to the Church's preaching does the will of God take effect in the world. On this view, the physical world contains its own principles of movement and causality and human agents act with genuine freedom. Far from postulating a divine cause behind each and every religiously significant event, the existentialist view rules out both obvious miracles and hidden interventions. Only at the point of the free decision of faith does talk of divine providence become possible. Trust in divine providence, on this view, is not a matter of believing that God is bringing about a certain sequence of events, or even a general trend in nature and history, but rather a matter of believing that, whatever happens, nothing can separate the man who trusts in God from God's presence and love. Events have their ordinary natural causes but, whatever happens, the man who trusts in God will be enabled to bring good out of evil, in virtue of the relation of grace and faith in which he stands. In other words, God's will takes effect in the world solely through the faith-response of those who trust him.

Paul Tillich expresses this view of providence in a well-known sermon:

> Faith in divine Providence is the faith that nothing can prevent us from fulfilling the ultimate meaning of our existence. Providence does not mean a divine planning by which everything is predetermined, as in an efficient machine. Rather, Providence means that there is a creative and saving possibility in every situation ...[2]

A similar view can be found in the writings of a number of modern theologians, not so influenced by continental existentialism, who are sometimes called 'perspectivists', from their tendency to treat religious language as expressing a certain *perspective* on the world. They suggest that talk of divine providence is not so much talk about special acts of God in the world, but rather a special way of talking about or looking at the things that happen in the world. All events fall within the broad scope of God's universal purpose, but some happen to bring to mind a special sense of the common divine purpose in all things. These we call providential, although, in doing so, we do not attribute them to the particular causality of God. Thus Professor Maurice Wiles writes: 'Talk of God's activity is, then, to be understood as a way of speaking about those events within the natural world or within human history in which God's purpose finds clear expression or special opportunity.'[3]

Such views, whether in their existentialist or perspectivist form, would clearly enable their holders to embrace the kind of explanation of evil which we have been exploring, and which relies

---

[2] Paul Tillich, 'The Meaning of Providence' in *The Shaking of the Foundations*. (Pelican 1962) p. 111.

[3] Maurice Wiles, *The Remaking of Christian Doctrine*. Cambridge University Press.

on the necessary role of creation through basic energies according to general laws. The basic difficulty with such views is precisely the fact that they seem to rule out the notion of God's action in nature and history, which is so central a feature of theism. They seem, in other words, to be advancing forms of deism. Existentialist theology may speak of an on-going relation of grace and faith experienced in the self-understanding of the believer, but as far as nature and history are concerned, it differs from deism only in refusing to talk about the relation between God and the natural world at all. And Professor Wiles admits explicitly that his position 'is deistic in so far as it refrains from claiming any effective causation on the part of God in relation to particular occurrences'.

THE HIDDEN HAND OF GOD

The question now arises for the reflective theist, whether these two positions, that of direct interventionism on the one hand, and that of existentialist theology or perspectivism on the other hand, are the only two options. Is there no middle way which might enable the theist to retain his theodicy in terms of the necessary conditions of personal life and growth and also to speak of divine providence in the sense of particular divine action in the world? Another way of putting the same question would be to ask whether it is possible at the same time to hold that the created universe has a given and regular structure, necessary for the production of persons, yet responsible for pain as well as good, and also to hold that that structure is flexible enough to allow for the divine inworking in a way which does not force or fake the natural operation of created energies and agencies.

A number of considerations might combine to support the view that there is such a middle way. In the first place the theory that all acts of God in the world are miracles, implying the divine invasion of a fixed natural system, is a highly implausible theory, even as an account of traditional belief. It is widely held in theistic religions that, whatever may be the case regarding miracles, God's normal mode of action is mediated, not direct. That is to say, most believers hold that God acts in and through

91

ordinary situations and ordinary people. The idea that God uses, say, a doctor or a priest or a child to bring about the healing or conversion of an individual is hardly foreign to religions such as Christianity. It is also widely held that historical traditions such as the faith of Israel, creative innovators such as the saints and doctors of the Church, books, sermons, sacramental actions—all of them explicable in natural terms—are also the vehicles of divine action in the world. Only a minority of believers would in fact regard every indication of God's care for their individual well-being as miraculous.

In the second place, where people claim to have discerned a providential pattern or development in history or in their own lives, such a providential thread will usually embrace suffering as well as prosperity and the activity of wicked men as well as good. Few would seriously suppose that God causes the evil in order to draw something creative out of it. We have already commented on the morally perverse character of such a supposition.

In the third place, it has been widely recognized, not only in the modern period, that it is improper, theologically speaking, to treat the activity of God as one causal factor on the same level, as it were, with other natural causal factors. Aquinas wrote very carefully about the relation between God's primary causality as the infinite source of the whole universe, and the secondary God-given causality of creatures. Modern theology has taken this insight further and recognized that in order to act within the structures of creation God need not be supposed to have to suspend or enhance the operation of the energies and agencies which he has made.

It would be a very odd picture of the relation between God and the world if the believer had to suppose that God could act in the world only by direct intervention. To suppose that he does so just occasionally would be to raise all the problems which perplex the believer as he reflects on the problem of evil, about why God does not intervene more often. It would also prevent him from appealing to the God-given structures of creation, and their necessary role in setting creatures at a distance from their creator and providing a stable environment for their lives, as an explanation for the physical ills which can afflict God's creatures.

Of course, if the created universe is also to be open to the hidden hand of God working in and through its energies and agencies without any faking or forcing of the natural causes, then it is no use thinking of the physical world as a rigidly deterministic system. The cosmos must have the flexibility to respond to the Spirit of God, as well as the orderly structure which constitutes a reliable environment. But on any view a rigidly mechanistic picture of the universe is quite impossible. We already have to postulate elements of spontaneity and a sufficiently flexible structure to permit the emergence of life and mind and free action on the part of creatures. It is not unreasonable to suppose further that the hidden hand of God can draw the many different threads of cause and effect together into new patterns in evolution, history and individual life, without suspending the natural order or forcing the natural sequence of events. The process becomes most clear to us, so the believer would say, when a living religious tradition enables men to come to know God personally and respond to him in faith and love. But at the same time the believer will have to admit that there are limits to what God can make of particular providential lines of development without breaking into the structures of creation and suspending operation of its laws. On the view under consideration this is precisely what he does not do, for very good reasons, which were explored in the last chapter, concerning the necessary role of some such structured physical world as this in the whole creative process. The fact that lives are sometimes stunted and cut short in the present phase of the creative process is not, of course, the end of the story, as we shall see in the next chapter.

Recognition of the limitation on providential activity imposed by the present structures of creation need not drive the believer to the opposite conclusion that there is no room for divine action in the world at all. On the contrary, it is open to him to hold that God is constantly at work in and through created structures, drawing the threads of human history and individual life into providential patterns. It is also open to the believer to suppose

93

that, even if God's present mode of action in the world is providential rather than miraculous, his future action in resurrection and recreation will be different; for, as we shall see in the next chapter, it is often held that God will transform the present structures of creation in the end. The Christian believer also holds that God has given mankind an anticipation of that future in the resurrection of Jesus from the dead. Such an exception to God's normal way of acting in and through the present structures of creation is not open to the arguments just reviewed, which object to the idea of occasional miraculous intervention. For the Christian, the resurrection of Jesus is a foretaste of all men's destiny.

The notion of divine providence sketched in this section has been most ably expounded and defended in the writings of the late Warden of Keble College, Oxford, Austin Farrer, some of whose books are mentioned in the bibliography.

7

THE OVERCOMING OF EVIL

Even if an acceptable idea of divine providence can be worked out, which at once allows the believer to speak of God's fatherly care for the world and for individual men and women, and also can explain the presence of evil in terms of the necessary role of physical structures, general laws, and human freedom in the creative process, there still remain some fundamental problems about the ultimate goal of the whole process. The two most searching questions which will occur to the reflective mind on surveying the practices, beliefs and arguments gathered together in this book, are, in the first place, what is this costly fashioning of persons leading up to, and, secondly, is any end-state involving such cost really worth it?

It is widely agreed among theists that our present experience of personal existence and relation cannot by itself justify the cost in suffering which the creative process entails. Notwithstanding the wonders and beauties of creation, and the profound and creative possibilities of human life, notwithstanding the intelligibility of some evil and suffering in a world capable of producing these goods, and notwithstanding the morally creative ways with which men can cope with suffering and evil, the whole process, as experienced so far, cannot realistically be held to make up for the untold pains and miseries which have as a matter of fact afflicted sentient and conscious beings on this planet since life began. If the universe is to be seen as the creation of an omnipotent and perfectly good God, then the believer must be prepared to speculate about the future goal of creation, where evil will be finally overcome, and in which the countless sufferers down the ages will themselves participate. It is difficult enough to see that such a future consummation will justify a process which involves so much past and present suffering. Without belief in some such consummation, however, the task of theodicy would seem to be an impossible one.

Before surveying briefly the ways in which the religions of the world have envisaged the ultimate destiny of man, it is perhaps worthwhile re-emphasizing the point that, if the arguments of chapters four and five have any weight, then the creation of a world of finite persons in relation with each other and with Gon necessarily takes the form of a gradual process. We may hazard the speculation that the spatio-temporal structure of our world is the necessary condition of finite personal being. It was argued in chapter six that only by beginning the creation with fundamental energies as it were at a distance from his own being, and building it up from the bottom, could the creator fashion a relatively independent context for finite personal life. Its self-reproducing and evolving nature, on this view, provides the kind of grounding over against God which gives the creature his own footing in reality and preserves his own finite being and nature. Once thus established in being he can become the object of the divine fatherly care and capable of the gift of whatever ultimate future God has in store for him. In a nutshell, the argument claimed that only by being fashioned in this creative process are finite persons there to be immortalized.

It needs to be kept in mind that such a picture would require us to treat the many stories coming to us out of the history of religions about an originally perfect creation or Golden Age as religious mythology, perhaps indicative of some intimation of the future goal of creation. For, on the view under consideration it is only in the ultimate future that the ills consequent upon the present order of the universe will be finally overcome.

NOTIONS OF MAN'S DESTINY IN TRIBAL AND ANCIENT RELIGIONS

Tribal religion has many myths of the original perfect state of creation. The Bambuti in the Congo, for instance, tell the story that 'God provided the first people with food, shelter, immortality and the gift of rejuvenating them when they grew old'.[1] But tribal religion appears to have little sense of any long-term

[1] John Mbiti, op. cit., p. 95.

future; we find no beliefs about historical progress (or decay), about the end of the world, or about a heavenly state. At death, the individual is held to persist for a while in the world of the spirits as long as he is remembered by name, but thereafter he fades away from existence. From this belief derives the importance of the symbolic offerings of food by which African families seek to keep their dead within the horizon of remembrance.

The classical world of Greece and Rome also has myths of original perfection. The myth of the Golden Age in Hesiod's poems, for example, portrays an ideal world in the past, where men 'lived like gods without sorrow of heart, remote and free from toil and grief' (*Works and Days* II. 112f). Even Plato took over these stories and gave them a more historical form in his myth of Atlantis, the island in the western sea, where, in perfect conditions, Plato's ideal city-state was held once upon a time to have been realized. The Greeks had little conception of an ultimate future for the universe, but they did develop cyclical conceptions of the world, whereby it would inexorably proceed through the ages of gold, silver, bronze and iron, and even when the golden age returned, it would only be the start of another cycle of decay. Virtuous mortals escaped this recurring cycle by being transported to the Isles of the Blest or the Elysian Fields, where they enjoyed eternal bliss.

THE DESTINY OF MAN AND THE WORLD IN EASTERN RELIGIONS

The basic pattern of Indian religious thought is a similar pattern of an endless cycle of birth and rebirth, from which a man might hope to gain release by ascetic, mystical or devotional concentration. The notion of a single ultimate goal of nature and history is alien to this tradition with its deep-seated belief in reincarnation. Just because the world is seldom seen as the divine creation, questions about its ultimate purpose and destiny seldom arise. It is true that Vaishnavism, with its doctrine of divine incarnations bringing help in times of special need, did produce the idea of a future Avatār, Kalkin, who would bring divine judgement and restore the golden age, but the idea is

97

hardly central even to this branch of devotional Hinduism.

We have seen how early Buddhism does not raise the kind of questions about creation, evil and the future which perplex the theist. Even in its many-sided developments, Mahāyāna Buddhism still maintained the fundamental notion of a way of enlightenment by which the individual could achieve Nirvāna. Nirvāna may be pictured differently in Pure Land Buddhism of China and Japan, where the Buddha Amida's compassion was held to have created a sphere of salvation into which his followers were drawn by grace, but there is no suggestion that the world of suffering from which men seek release has itself a necessary role in the overall economy of creation. For there is no doctrine of creation, or of the world itself as a meaningful and goal-directed process.

One might have expected the pure monotheism of the Sikhs to contain beliefs in creation and the consummation of creation more akin to those of the western theistic religions, but in fact Sikhism retains its Indian roots in seeing salvation as release from illusory worldly values into harmony with the divine order and union with God. There is no explanation, in the sense in which western theists look for an explanation of evil and suffering, for the place of suffering in the world. Least of all is there any recognition of the necessary role of a world containing the possibility of suffering as part of a process leading to an ultimate goal.

The idea of paradise, however, is a recurrent motif in religious thought even in the east. We have just seen how it appears in the Pure Land schools of Mahāyāna Buddhism. Similar developments occurred earlier in China in the case of the ancient mystical religion of Taoism. Just as its quietist nature mysticism came in the course of time to attract more popular magical ideas and practices, so it developed a belief in the Isles of the Blest, where men live on flowers and never die. Taoism is in any case an optimistic way, lacking a sense of profound and radical evil. The kind of questions which perplex the theist do not arise here any more than they do in the case of Buddhism.

The development of the faith of Israel from that of a tribal religion to a universal faith was a long process. At first the people of Israel believed themselves to have a special historical destiny of their own. Only later did their role as a light to the nations acquire pre-eminence. Two further developments need special notice. Their historical experience of recurrent disaster led to the growth of belief in a divine judgement, a day of the Lord, when God would decisively intervene. Sometimes the hope is more of this-worldly perfection under a Davidic king: 'The wolf shall dwell with the lamb ... they shall not hurt nor destroy in all my holy mountain; for the earth shall be full of the knowledge of the Lord as the waters cover the sea' (Isa. 11. 6, 9).

At the same time, the problem of innocent suffering and martyrdom led to the characteristically Jewish belief in resurrection. By the time of Jesus, acceptance of the idea of a general resurrection in the last day was widespread. Modern Judaism, except in its secularized forms, retains the expectation of the coming of a personal Messiah, and the belief in general resurrection. Only in the light of such belief in the eventual vindication of his people can Jewish faith in God retain its force in the face of the terrible sufferings of the Jews.

Christianity began with faith in Jesus Christ risen from the dead. His resurrection was seen as the guarantee and foretaste of the general resurrection in the last day, and the hope of a glorious resurrection became one of the corner stones of Christian belief as enshrined in the creeds. At first regarded as imminent and expected within the lifetime of the first Christians, the day of resurrection soon came to be thought of as the final (and distant) moment of divine intervention in winding up the history of the world, and bestowing the gift of eternal life on all those redeemed by Jesus Christ. Of course, eternal life was also thought of as the dimension of spiritual relationship to God into which the believer could enter here and now, but the future hope was never lost sight of. Indeed, the destiny of man was held to be, in Augustine's words, to know God and enjoy him for ever. Christian art down the centuries has portrayed in innumerable ways the day of judgement, the torments of the lost, the fires of purgation, and the bliss of the beatific vision in heaven. In this final overcoming of all evil, it has been believed, the creative purposes of God will reach their culmination and the sufferings of this present life will be seen to have been worthwhile. This faith has never been better expressed than in the book of Revelation: 'Then I saw a new heaven and a new earth ... and I heard a great voice from the throne saying "Behold, the dwelling of God is with men. He will dwell with them; and they shall be his people, and God himself will be with them; he will wipe away every tear from their eyes, and death shall be no more, neither shall there be mourning nor crying nor pain any more, for the former things have passed away." And he who sat upon the throne said, "Behold I make all things new."' (21.1–5).

The Qur'ān also speaks of the resurrection of the dead and the day of judgement. Both heaven and hell are vigorously described (as in the later Christian tradition). The Muslim heaven is pictured very sensuously as a garden of bliss and peace, which later Islamic thought spiritualized and treated symbolically.

COPING WITH EVIL AND EXPLAINING EVIL

It can be seen, then, that the religions of the world have had a marked tendency to develop ideas of resurrection and a future life, in which men and women pass beyond the range of evil and enter upon a state of bliss that makes all their sufferings worthwhile. This tendency is particularly strong in the case of the monotheistic world religions, but it is to be seen also wherever the note of personal devotion comes to the fore in an otherwise mystical or non-theistic religion. We can see how such beliefs can help men both to cope with suffering and evil in this present life, and also to explain, if not the presence of suffering and evil in the world, then at least the worthwhileness of creation despite the world's ills.

In chapter two we distinguished five ways of coping with

suffering and evil exemplified to different degrees and in different combinations by the religions of the world. Of those five ways, only the way of mystical knowledge is essentially independent of a future hope. Admittedly, in conjunction, say, with Christian faith mystical experience has been thought of as a foretaste of heavenly bliss, but in most religions the mystical state in itself, whether interpreted as union with God or with the Absolute, or as the isolation of the pure self, is sufficient as a way out of human suffering. Not so the other ways. More often than not, the way of renunciation and way of works have been practised in the interests of a higher heavenly reward. Even when this somewhat mercenary attitude to discipline and goodness has been transcended, and human goodness thought of rather as the natural consequence of the faith-response to God, it has still been widely felt that God must have an eternal destiny in mind for his personal creatures. Thus we have seen the way of devotion, in the monotheistic faiths, developing strong doctrines of resurrection or immortality. Similarly it has not been possible, in the context of devotional religion, to see the way of sacrifice as an ultimate end in itself. Whatever may be the case with the Bodhisattva who sacrificed himself to feed the hungry tigress, in the monotheistic faiths self-sacrifice is not the end. Jewish, Christian and Muslim martyrs have gone to their deaths in the confident hope of resurrection. There is no doubt, then, that this pervasive feature of religion has contributed greatly to the manner in which men and women have been enabled to cope with suffering and evil.

It has also helped them to make sense of the world as the creation of a good and all-powerful God. Taken in conjunction with the various ways of explaining the presence of evil in the world, which we examined in chapter three, the hope of resurrection, whether thought of crudely in terms of reward, or more spiritually in terms of insight into God's ultimate destiny for man, creates a new perspective in which to judge the worthwhileness of creation. Moreover the more convincingly one can show that the risks of present evil are a necessary condition of the fashioning of persons separate from God, the more plausible will be the claim that the ultimate consummation of God's creative process will be seen to justify the whole enterprise, despite the suffering and evil.

HEAVEN AND HELL

The widespread belief in the eternal damnation of the wicked in hell, which in one form or another characterizes most theistic traditions, militates against such an optimistic conclusion. Admittedly, from time to time, particularly in the history of Christianity, we find the belief that *all* men will in the end be saved—the view known as universalism—but it is a minority view, and the larger part even of Christian teaching about 'the last things' includes the doctrine that men have the freedom and the power to reject God and cut themselves off from him through all eternity. Their fate is vividly pictured in the art and literature of Christendom, as of other religious traditions, concerning the day of judgement.

The possibility of hell is often held to demonstrate the dignity and seriousness of human moral choice. Thus T. S. Eliot wrote: 'It is true to say that the glory of man is his capacity for salvation; it is also true to say that his glory is his capacity for damnation'. But just as we have seen reason in earlier chapters for the reflective theist to treat the devil as a symbolic figure for all that opposes God in the human world, so now similar considerations will support the view that hell and eternal punishment are also figurative and symbolic notions, and do not literally describe permanent aspects of reality in the final consummation of the divine purpose. For a permanent or eternal sphere of malice and rebellion and suffering is not conceivable as part of the ultimate destiny of creation. It makes neither metaphysical, moral nor religious sense. Metaphysically speaking, the theist is bound to suppose that the final state of created being will be good without qualification, and the existence of hell would undoubtedly introduce a major permanent qualification. Morally speaking, the idea of eternal punishment has to be rejected by the sensitive moral conscience quite independently of religion. But also religiously speaking, at any rate the Christian moral conscience, if it is really responsive to the love

102

of God claimed to be revealed in Jesus Christ, cannot in consistency tolerate the literal idea of hell.

If the literal idea of hell is rejected, the question remains, what does the language of hell and damnation in scripture and tradition symbolize? There seem to be two possibilities for the rational theist. Either he must affirm universalism, and hold that in God's eternity all men will be won over and saved. In this case the language of hell and damnation will certainly symbolize the horror of existence turned in upon the self and alienated from God, but it will not be regarded as portraying a permanent actuality. Among the Fathers of the Christian Church, Origen claimed that 'Christ remains on the Cross so long as the last sinner remains in hell', the implication being that the patience of God is such as to wait upon the repentance and renewal of all men in God's future. This is undoubtedly a morally and religiously attractive view.

However, it may be an over-optimistic view. It may be that the theist will have to admit that if freedom is to be real, it must be possible for a man to persist in the rejection of God, and so to embrace evil that he renders himself incapable of redemption. In such a case, one could only suppose that there is no point in God's keeping him in being. Such a man will be 'lost eternally' only in the sense that he has made himself incapable of taking part in God's future, and therefore suffers annihilation. The language of hell would in this case be taken to symbolize the awesome possibility of such an ultimate loss.

In either case—that of universalism or the annihilation of the irredeemable—there can be no permanent state of real being which remains in rebellion against God through all eternity. Consequently it is possible to hold that the absolute good of the transformed and perfected creation will in the end be seen to justify the total creative process despite its inevitable risks and temporary evils.

THE CONSUMMATION OF ALL THINGS

The manner in which the end state of creation is pictured in the scriptures and religious literature of the world varies greatly.

Sometimes, as we have seen, it is misplaced as characterizing an original state of perfection or Golden Age in the past. When it is more plausibly located in the future, it is sometimes pictured very vividly, indeed sensuously, as in the Qur'ān, and sometimes in the negative language of, say, Christian mysticism. Sometimes the characterization is very moving in its simplicity as in Isaiah's portrayal of God's holy mountain, where 'they shall neither hurt nor destroy' or in the book of Revelation's vision of the heavenly Jerusalem, where God 'will wipe away every tear from their eye'. The wider Christian tradition has developed the theme in many directions. Some modes of picturing heaven may well seem unattractive, but a work of the imaginative power of Dante's 'Paradiso' can perhaps indicate something of the sublimity of the Christian hope of the beatific vision. There has, admittedly, been a persistent tendency to belittle the significance of the material creation in Christian speculation about heaven. To take mystical experience as the clue to an understanding of heaven may be to fail to do justice to the goodness of the present structures of creation and to the hope that it is this world and not some other which will be transformed into the resurrection-world.

Nevertheless, religious agnosticism about God's ultimate plans for the created universe is an inevitable stance for the reflective theist. Our knowledge of the physical world is such that we cannot assume an uninterrupted evolutionary progress into a perfected future state. According to the second law of thermo-dynamics, whatever may be the case with local systems of energy like the solar system and the life it sustains, the ultimate state of the cosmos will be the dissipation of ordered structures through the 'heat-death of the universe'. Consequently, whatever the believer says about the providence of God working in and through the structures of creation in its present phase, he must suppose some future recreative divine act of transformation or resurrection, if the final state of the creation is to be thought of as free from its present limitations.

This being so, the believer is bound to be agnostic about the form which the ultimate state of God's creation will take. He can only trust in the love of God which he believes to have been revealed and, in the light of his present experience of God, affirm with Julian of Norwich that 'all shall be well, and all shall be well, and all manner of thing shall be well'.

Speculation about the transformed and perfected state of God's creation inevitably raises again the question why, if such a state is possible in the end, does not God create it directly, without going through the long drawn out and costly process in which we are now participating. If a heaven free from evil and suffering and from all the limitations of the present order is a real possibility, why is it not brought into being at once? The answer can only be along the lines of the argument of chapter five, namely that the gradualness of the creative process from the simplest energies up to life and personal being is a necessary condition of the establishment of persons in being over against God. Once they are there in being and have been given the chance to grow and develop as free agents in an environment relatively independent of the creator, then they can be drawn into relation with God and in due course immortalized. Only by some such process can the children of God be brought into being and nurtured and trained for eternity.

A further point may now be added. One of the functions of the evolving natural universe was to be the soil in which self-reproducing creatures could multiply, without the constant intervention of God. In Austin Farrer's words, God 'makes the creatures make themselves'. In heaven, the believer may suppose, there are no new persons. The 'new' creation is rather the resurrection of those originally fashioned in the mould of the present universe.

IVAN'S QUESTION ONCE AGAIN

At the end of our survey of the different practical and theoretical responses to suffering and evil, which the religions of the world have developed, the believer remains confronted by the question which Ivan Karamazov put to his brother Alyosha in Dostoevsky's novel. The believer is bound to ask himself if he would consent to create a world of life and growth and eventual happiness at such a cost. It may be that the wonder and beauty of creation, culminating in the life of persons, necessitates that combination of order and flexibility which makes for harm as well as good, and for the freedom which can be so terribly abused. It may be that God can and does draw good out of evil in countless remarkable ways, particularly, according to Christian belief, in and through his own self-involvement to the point of crucifixion. It may be that in the end God will, by an act of sovereign recreation, bestow upon his creatures the gift of eternal happiness. But even if these things are so, there still remains the problem of the cost in human suffering and wickedness here on earth.

It is very hard to reach a balanced view on this problem. We are, after all, on the theistic view, in the midst of the process of creation, and the significance of history as a whole can hardly be recognized, let alone assessed, until the historical process is complete. We are also finite creatures, endowed with very limited vision, and apt to jump to unjustified conclusions. We may understand why Ivan returns his entrance ticket, but it may be a premature and unbalanced action all the same. The believer may feel that some of the considerations presented in this book, especially the argument that creation *has* to take some such form as this, show that it is at least morally possible for him to accept the universe, to thank God for his existence, and to trust in the ultimate overcoming of evil in the end.

Appendix

ANIMALS

The pains of animals have often been felt to be a special problem for the sensitive religious mind. This is particularly so in the theistic religions, since it is very hard to fathom God's purpose in creating an animal world that can so easily be viewed as 'red in tooth in claw'. Buddhism, despite its recognition of the suffering of all living beings, does not consider this a problem for the understanding. As we have seen, Buddhism concentrates on the way for men to escape the fate of perpetual suffering which they share with the animal world.

It is also true that western theism has tended to foster this sensitivity to animal pain much more than eastern theism. The reason for this is that in Judaism, Christianity and Islam the overwhelming emphasis has been on man and man's position as the culmination of God's creation. Eastern religion, by contrast, has seen the animal and human worlds as bound up together in a single universe of life. According to the Indian doctrine of reincarnation, the accumulation of 'bad *karma*' may well lead to rebirth in the animal world. It is believed that the god Vishnu more than once appeared on earth as an animal Avatār.

In western theism, with its concentration on personal being, on the love of God, and on personal response to God as the chief end of creation, the purpose and function of animals have become obscure, and the pains of animals particularly hard to justify. The Christian believer, for example, is bound to experience doubts about the character of the subhuman world in which animals prey on one another and fall victim to parasitic organisms, about the apparent wastefulness of nature's prodigality in spawning multitudes of sentient organisms which never reach maturity, and about the apparent wastefulness of the whole evolutionary process by which the different species up to man have emerged. It is also the case that the alien nature of many insects, of strange creatures in the depths of the ocean, and of the lumbering prehistoric monsters, can come to cast doubt upon a religious view of the world.

Nevertheless it is animal pain that troubles the believer most. It is also the basis of much unbelief. In a pessimistic poem of great beauty, Thomas Hardy bewails the very birth of sentience in the natural world:

A time there was, as one may guess
And as, indeed, earth's testimonies tell,
Before the birth of consciousness,
When all went well.

None suffered sickness, love or loss,
None knew regret, starved hope, or heart-burnings,
None cared whatever crash or cross
Brought wrack to things.

If something ceased no tongue bewailed,
If something winced and waned, no heart was wrung,
If brightness dimmed and dark prevailed,
No sense was stung.

But the disease of feeling germed
And primal rightness took the tinct of wrong;
'Ere nescience shall be reaffirmed
How long, how long, how long, how long?

In this poem Hardy uses the language of the Christian doctrine of the fall to characterize the emergence not only of consciousness but of feeling—sentience—in the world, and longs for the day when there will be no more life on earth.

Such a negative view is hard to sustain. The believer might attempt to reply to all these objections along the following lines.

It is possible that personal theism overemphasizes the significance and place of man in the universe. God may be thought to have other purposes too in bringing into being an almost infinitely various world of animal life with all its energy, vitality and beauty. It is also possible that man views the animal world too anthropomorphically. Some forms of life strike human beings as alien only because they tend to think of all living beings by

108

analogy with themselves. To adopt the naturalist's approach to animals and insects as objects of interest and study in their own right is to abandon such anthropomorphic thinking. C. S. Lewis wrote that he lost his fear of spiders as soon as he developed a naturalist's interest in them. Similarly a cat's playing with a captured bird horrifies because of the apparent analogy with human cruelty. In fact the concept of cruelty cannot be appropriately applied outside the sphere of human intentional acts.

It is also possible for personal theistic religious traditions to come to value the animal creation for its own sake. Thus the Hebrew Bible sees life itself as good. In the book of Genesis living beings in the sea, on the earth and in the air are created and commanded to be fruitful and to multiply, and 'God saw that it was good'. In the book of Job the greatness of God is manifested in his creation, among other things, of the monsters of the deep. Job's picture of God is shown up as having been too small.

The pains of animals have to be understood in the same way as the pains of man. Pain has the same necessary function, and, as has already been seen, an organic world of self-reproducing creatures has necessary limitations. The conditions of life and growth and sensitivity and of the wonders and beauties of the animal world are at the same time the conditions of accident, hurt, disease and death. You cannot have the one without the other. Our growing understanding of ecology shows how right Aquinas was to see in the conditions of the balance of nature the necessity of pain and death. Human beings need, of course, to remember that the animals do not suffer the pangs of reflection and anticipation which increase the sum of human ills.

Notwithstanding what was said above about the many-sided nature of the divine purpose in creating a world of life, it remains the case that, if the believer is right to think of God as creating the whole universe from the bottom up in and through the fundamental energies and systems of the natural world, without any faking or forced intervention, then we should expect to find a prodigality of natural forms of life, out of which a human personal world can emerge. If God is to 'make the creature make itself' we cannot expect constant interference, ruling out unnecessary developments and experiments in forms of life. In his infinite wisdom and patience God lets every conceivable form of life develop and enjoy its own vitality, however brief. At the same time this whole teeming world of life is the forge in which God's personal creatures are fashioned, the soil from which they emerge.

William Blake expressed something of the strangeness and the wonder of the animal creation in his poem on the tiger:

> Tyger Tyger, burning bright,
> In the forests of the night;
> What immortal hand or eye,
> Could frame thy fearful symmetry?
>
> What the hammer? what the chain?
> In what furnace was thy brain?
> What the anvil? what dread grasp,
> Dare its deadly terrors clasp?
>
> When the stars threw down their spears
> And watered heaven with their tears:
> Did he smile his work to see?
> Did he who made the Lamb make thee?

These are some of the considerations which may enable the believer to adopt a more positive view of the world of sentient and conscious life than that expressed in Thomas Hardy's poem. The Christian believer may also find himself driven to affirm, with the medieval theologian Peter Abelard, that the cross of Christ reveals the suffering in the heart of God which all creation entails for the creator. There we see him taking on himself not only the wickedness and suffering of man, but also the pains of all his creatures. The cross, it might be argued, manifests in time the suffering of God throughout the creative process until it is complete.

BIBLIOGRAPHY

Bowker, J. W., *Problems of Suffering in Religions of the World*, C.U.P. 1970.

Eliade, M., *Myths, Dreams and Mysteries*, Fontana 1968.

Farrer, A. M., *Faith and Speculation*, A. & C. Black 1967.

Farrer, A. M., *Love Almighty and Ills Unlimited*, Collins 1962.

Farrer, A. M., *A Science of God?* Bles 1966.

Hick, J. H., *Evil and the God of Love*, Macmillan 1966.

Klostermaier, K., *Hindu and Christian in Vrindaban*, S.C.M. 1969.

McCloskey, H. J., *God and Evil*, Martinus Nijhoff, The Hague, 1974.

Ling, T. O., *A History of Religion East and West*, Macmillan 1968.

Parrinder, G., *Man and his Gods—encyclopaedia of the world's religions*, Hamlyn 1971.

Pike, N., ed., *God and Evil*, Prentice-Hall 1964.

Plantinga, A., *God, Freedom and Evil*, Allen and Unwin 1975.

Simon, U., *A Theology of Auschwitz*, Gollancz 1967.

Smart, N., *Philosophers and Religious Truth*, chapter VI. S.C.M. 2nd edn. 1969.

Smart, N., *The Religious Experience of Mankind*, Fontana 1971.

Tennant, F. R., *Philosophical Theology Vol. II*, C.U.P. 1937.

INDEX

Abelard, P., 110
Albigenses, the, 44f.
Al Hallaj, 28
animals, 3, 5, 11, 43, 86, 107-110
Anthony, St, 23
Aquinas, 58f., 63, 72ff., 92, 109
Aristotle, 19
asceticism, 1, 21-24, 27, 43
Augustine, 44, 46, 54, 57f., 63, 69, 99
Auschwitz, 50, 63, 66

Berger, P., 12
Bhagavad Gītā, 22, 26, 29f., 33ff.
Blake, W., 110
Bodhisattvas, 4, 30, 32, 35, 38, 41, 84
Bowker, J. W., 38
Buddhism, 1-5, 7-11, 12, 15f., 21ff., 26f., 29f., 34f., 38, 40f., 46f., 55, 84f., 98, 101, 107

Calvin, 57, 63
Camus, A., 15ff., 37
China, 16, 21, 23, 27, 30, 35, 41, 98
Christianity, 6-13, 21, 23, 27ff., 31, 36, 38f., 44, 46ff., 49ff., 54, 57, 63f., 67, 69ff., 86f., 92, 94, 99, 101f., 104, 106ff., 110
Confucius, 23, 35

Dante, 104
deism, 82f.
determinism, 20, 61, 93
devil, the, 45, 48f., 52f., 59, 70f., 79, 102
Dionysus, 20
Dostoevsky, F., 5ff., 9, 11, 13, 52f., 64ff., 81, 105f.
drugs, 29
dualism, 24, 35, 42-45, 70

Eckhart, 28
Eliade, M., 85
Eliot, T. S., 102
Epicurus, 14f.
Erasmus, 57
Essenes, the, 23
existentialism, 89ff.

Farrer, A., 94, 105
Feuerbach, L., 88
Flavel, J., 87f.
Francis, St, 24, 36
free will, 10, 51ff., 55-67, 68, 70, 72, 75, 79, 82, 89, 95

Galen, 72
Greek religion, 19ff., 37, 42, 83, 97

114

Also published by Sheldon Press

ISSUES IN RELIGIOUS STUDIES
General Editors: Peter Baelz and Jean Holm

The Nature of Belief

Elizabeth Maclaren

Some people already know where they stand on the question of belief. They believe or disbelieve confidently, and are rarely moved to consider any alternative position. Others find it more difficult, see something to be said for most of the arguments, but nothing conclusive for any, and oscillate between belief and unbelief. In so far as this book has a stance, it is nearer the latter position than the former. It will not *settle* the question of the nature of belief, but it will try to explore it as open-mindedly as possible.

The author sets out for discussion the various aspects of belief that must be examined if we are to understand the word in its fullest sense: whether we believe out of habit, because of the evidence or in spite of it; what we believe, how our beliefs can change, and how we can be changed by our beliefs.

'This study is well balanced, businesslike, and well illustrated with wide-ranging quotations.'

The Times Educational Supplement

Also published by Sheldon Press

ISSUES IN RELIGIOUS STUDIES
General Editors: Peter Baelz and Jean Holm

Religious Language

Peter Donovan

Modern study of religions reminds us that they are not just a matter of words; yet words play a crucial role in their claims to truth. Dr Donovan has written a lucid introduction to the thinking that philosophers of religion have done in recent years about the way religions use language, what the claims made by religious believers mean, and how questions about the truth of those claims can be considered. The challenge of natural, non-religious thinking to religion to show how its oblique, often obscure, claims can count as factual rather than fictional, forms the central issue. Questions about the content and truth of religious statements are seen in the wider context of experience, worship, behaviour, and traditions of religious authority.

'Dr Donovan's scholarly book is written in deceptively simple prose, but is, as the subject-matter demands, closely reasoned. His argument is illustrated with numerous well-chosen citations from contemporary professional philosophers, and his examples of religious language are culled from other religions as well as Christianity.'

The Times Educational Supplement

Also published by Sheldon Press

ISSUES IN RELIGIOUS STUDIES
General Editors: Peter Baelz and Jean Holm

The Worlds of
Science and Religion

Don Cupitt

To what extent has science destroyed religion? The author
admits that in modern, science-based cultures the old religious
cosmology has been underminded to such an extent that we no
longer have a firmly based moral order. He discusses the future
of a society which has no inherent values and whether a scientific
standpoint can coexist with, or be a substitute for, a religious
code.

In successive chapters he explores philosophical questions about
Darwinism, the peculiar features of the science-religion issue in
Christianity, religious and non-religious cosmologies, the rise of
the sciences of man, determinism, technology and ritual, religious
and scientific knowledge and the place of science in society.

Also published by Sheldon Press

ISSUES IN RELIGIOUS STUDIES
General Editors: Peter Baelz and Jean Holm

Interpreting the Bible

David Stacey

The author has taught the Bible for twenty years and during that time he has gained considerable experience in dealing with the really knotty questions of interpretation that arise. His concern is to help those starting a serious study of the Bible not to pre-judge the fundamental questions raised by such a study but to confront them squarely. This is not always a straightforward matter. The Bible is an ancient book from a culture far removed from our own, yet it is held by many to be significant for our time. How can we translate the multifarious literature of Judaism and primitive Christianity into the language of our present urban society so that the Bible does in fact speak relevantly? Dr Stacey considers methods and approaches which have been used to interpret the Bible through history to the present day.

'Punchy vigour and clarity characterize this new series.'
Church of England Newspaper

Also published by Sheldon Press

Five books which introduce the wisdom of various groups of mystics and then give a wide selection of their stories, sayings, poems and anecdotes.

The Wisdom of the Desert
THOMAS MERTON

The Wisdom of the Zen Masters
IRMGARD SCHLOEGL
Foreword by Christmas Humphreys

The Wisdom of the Forest
Sages of the Indian Upanishads
GEOFFREY PARRINDER

The Wisdom of the Jewish Mystics
ALAN UNTERMAN

The Wisdom of the Sufis
KENNETH CRAGG

If you would would like a complete list of the books published by Sheldon Press, please write to the Editorial Department, Sheldon Press, SPCK Building, Marylebone Road, London NW1 4DU.